PERIOD?

PERIOD?

LIFE WITH MENSTRUATION

Enjoy!

— Miriam P

MIRIAM PROSNITZ

NDP

NEW DEGREE PRESS

COPYRIGHT © 2021 MIRIAM PROSNITZ

PERIOD?

Life with Menstruation

ISBN   978-1-63730-344-3   *Paperback*

978-1-63730-345-0   *Kindle Ebook*

978-1-63730-346-7   *Ebook*

CONTENTS

CONTENTS

AUTHOR'S NOTE

When I hit puberty, my vagina went from something that could be ignored because it basically didn't exist to this hairy living creature that needed to breathe and leaked blood and cervical mucus. Kind of like a werewolf with a head cold—it was a pretty impressive if gruesome transformation.

I was understandably distraught by my new moon howler, but thankfully I had a sister who knew exactly how to handle my situation. When I went into the bathroom to pee, she'd follow me in. Weird? Maybe to your unascendant mind, but to my sister, these bathroom chats were the path to enlightenment. This exposure therapy, double entendre intended, would make me comfortable with my new body. Did it work? I didn't think so for a long time, but recently I needed a new hobby and decided writing a book about vaginas would be a great idea, so it must have done something. Normal people get to pee in private and don't later write books about vaginas. Thanks, Hannah!

In case you didn't have a sister who followed you into the toilet, I wrote this book for you. I know menstruation is an uncomfortable topic for many, so this book is going to help you *get the fuck over it*. I'm not saying you're going to marvel in pure delight at the first tremor of an oncoming cramp, but knowing more about menstruation and the variety of women's experiences can save us all a lot of time and pain.

You might think I'm exaggerating, but we've been dealing with a lack of female anatomy education and the ensuing problems for a long time. The first-ever crisis hotline was founded in response to a young girl committing suicide after her genitals began to bleed. She didn't know about menstruation (Samaritans, 2010). It's been over sixty-five years since then, and girls and women everywhere still struggle with a lack of basic knowledge about their bodies, leading to hygiene problems, unwanted pregnancies, and a rise in labiaplasty (cosmetic surgery of the labia). We all need to be better at talking about our bodies to improve things for the next generation, the young girls of today.

That said, this book is *not* for little girls. Please, dear heavens, do not give this book to your five-year-old niece. If my own niece were to read this Author's Note before the age of sixteen, my head would turn the color of fresh menstrual blood, a.k.a. Louboutin red, and explode. In case you doubt me and still think this would be a good holiday gift for your young relatives, you should be aware we'll be covering topics including vaginal odor, masturbation, and period sex (the ultimate stocking stuffer).

Through this material, you can see and learn from the vast range of experiences women have with their bodies, period products, families, friends, and partners. Some relationships are truly precious, while some *suck*, and it's healthy to acknowledge the differences and see them in action. (Note on these differences, the partners who suck don't usually suck if you catch my drift.) This book is jammed full of action you can learn from, both in the metaphorical and literal sense (and unlike the high school health class you took when you were still a virgin, this time you may actually learn something).

While this book is about women and their menstrual experiences, it's meant for everyone *(except children)*. This book is for all women who struggled the first time they inserted a tampon or told a male colleague they had a headache when it was actually cramps. It's also for the men whose female friends get *headaches* surprisingly often. It's not an educational book in the traditional sense. It's a collection of fictional short stories speaking truth to periods.

You're probably wondering why someone who, before writing this book, didn't know the difference between the vulva and the vagina is qualified to speak truth to periods. I would argue my lack of formal qualifications makes me a perfect person to dive into the taboo and minutia around menstruation. To my utter relief, I am not a doctor. Being a doctor is hard and involves memorizing a lot of fancy terminologies. Even the word *terminologies* is fancy. I won't use fancy words you don't know or assume you know things you don't. Hell, before doing research for this book, I didn't know the difference between the vulva and the vagina. It turns out the vulva are the sadly ignored bits on the outside, while the vagina is a three to six-inch hole which no one ever measures—even though every man on earth has seemingly measured his dick. I also had no clue which period product was approved for mess-free sex. (If you're wondering, it's the menstrual disk, though no one has ever heard of it, and many people have sex with tampons or menstrual cups inserted. People who want to have sex will have sex, "screw" what's already inside their vagina). It's okay that we don't know these things. No one ever taught us.

You and I are starting at the same baseline knowledge, except I've probably had a peculiar preoccupation with female anatomy for a longer period of time than you. At seventeen, a college application asked me to tell them about something I had read, and I kid you not, I wrote about vaginas. The first sentence of my response was, "Sometime last year I read a news article about how, for the first time, female primates are experiencing the symptoms of menopause." Yes, gorilla periods got me into college.* As I hope you can see, I've written this book from a place of longstanding genuine curiosity and a desire to learn, and I hope you will learn alongside me.

In preparation to write this book, I spoke to dozens of women about their experiences with menstruation. Therefore, these *fictional* stories are amalgamations of the experiences of real girls and women. Everyone experiences menstruation differently, and I wanted this book to reflect that. Sometimes it's funny—like the awkward moment when someone accidentally inserts a tampon, forgetting they already had a tampon in their vagina. Sometimes it's bizarre or cringeworthy, like when a man becomes judgmental or controlling of a woman's choice of birth control. But no matter what, these stories are all meant to be honest. They show different perspectives on being a woman living her life while also wrangling her moon howler. If you haven't figured it out yet, this book isn't really about periods. It's about women.

If you're a woman, do something for yourself, for the women in your life, and for me (a fellow female), and recommend this book to a dozen of your *adult* friends. Menstruate and not a woman? I hope you can enjoy these stories as well. Not someone who has ever menstruated? Buy two dozen copies and then give them to other nonmenstruating people.

Just because you don't have a vagina doesn't mean you should shut like a clam when the topic comes up. Instead, leave your emotional clam open and enjoy the slippery smooth ride. Seriously, these stories are meant to be accessible, and you shouldn't be scared (but if you are scared that's okay too, as long as you buy *three* dozen copies). This book should make you laugh, cry, and be absolutely disgusted. Like so grossed out you're tempted to put the book down, but you can't because sometimes life is like a car crash you just *can't stop looking at*. If not, I have failed.

In conclusion, fuck the vagina taboo. Knowledge is power. Now get reading!

*For your benefit, I've included the prompt and short answer essay seventeen-year-old Miriam submitted to Cooper Union in her college application. Note I did not attend Cooper Union, but they did accept me in spite of this submission.

Tell us about something you have read (i.e., book, article, journal, etc.) and your thoughts about it:

Sometime last year I read a news article about how, for the first time, female primates are experiencing the symptoms of menopause. In the wild, female primates do not live long enough to experience menopause. However, in captivity these animals are outliving their wild counterparts and experiencing the same symptoms of old age as human women. Since I am a curious person, I found this article fascinating and odd. It speaks to how our actions, keeping the primates in captivity, have consequences both good and bad. While living longer may be viewed as good, I cannot imagine that a chimp or gorilla in the zoo experiencing hot flashes makes for a happy animal or zookeeper!

CHAPTER ONE

THE MENSTRUAL CYCLE

———

Be twelve. Get your period before the bus ride home. Think you pooped your pants. You don't have time to deal with pooped pants because you're going to miss your bus. Plus, you don't remember pooping your pants. Rub at the lining of your panda patterned underwear with thin one-ply toilet paper. Sniff the toilet paper like a dog examining a particularly interesting patch of grass. Poo doesn't usually smell metallic and usually isn't in the front of your underwear. This is blood. Worry that you're dying for approximately three seconds. Realize this is the alleged *menstrual blood*. This *blood* is not as red as you were expecting. Celebrate not pooing your pants for approximately one second. Panic that you have your first period while wearing light blue pants. Stuff additional one-ply toilet paper in your underwear. Dismiss the toilet paper as a one-time solution, but you're definitely wrong.

Run to the bus. Because you're the last one, you're forced to sit next to a *boy*. Even worse, it's the overly talkative boy who always smells like bologna. Someone nearby, another boy who definitely has cooties, is wearing too much Axe body spray, and the scents mix in a disgusting concoction.

You may want to vomit but don't. Instead, distract yourself from vomiting by talking to the boy sitting next to you. This conversation has the added advantage of making you feel superior since most twelve-year-old girls are terrible people who never talk to this boy because he's not *cool*. You're a better person than the other girls. Pray to Jesus if you cross your legs tight enough, your period will stop. You're a good person, so Jesus should listen to you. Bologna boy asks if you're going to pee yourself. You shake your head no and cross your legs tighter. He tells the rest of the bus you're about to pee yourself. The other girls cackle at you like hyenas.

Get off the bus; run to your house. Try to forget the echo of all the girls laughing as you shove more two-ply toilet paper in your underwear. Find your mom. Wish you had a cool mom. You don't have a cool mom. Tell your mom about your period in as few words as possible. Don't mention bologna boy or the hyena cackling. Mom gives you a super absorbent jumbo-pad with wings. The pad is larger than your underwear and the wings, which are supposed to stick to the fabric, instead crinkle and rub at your legs. Walk like a penguin to minimize friction. Thankfully your mom takes you to the grocery store and lets you pick out new pads. You pick out less-jumbo pads without wings and then hide by the swooshing automatic doors while your mom checks out. These new pads roll around in your underwear until every pair you own is stained.

By the time you're fourteen, all the girls in your gym class wear thongs while you're still wearing blood-stained briefs. Buy thongs at the mall with your best friend using babysitting money. Hope your mom won't notice them in the laundry. You dislike the constant wedgie your new underwear gives you, but like that you can now fart silently. Blame your silent farts on the dog. Everyone comments on how old the dog is getting, and your mom looks into new dog food. Get your period. Try wearing a pad with your thong. Girls in the changing room laugh at you. Steal a jumbo plus tampon from your mom's bathroom while she's busy cooking. Try getting the tampon in without success. Google "how to insert a tampon." Watch a YouTube tutorial. Angle the tampon correctly. Shove the tampon in. Squirm and waddle around for an hour until dinner. Shove hot food down your throat while your mom attempts to ask about your day. Run to the bathroom. Pull the tampon out while it's still dry, causing horrible vaginal rug burns. From now on, stick to brief-style underwear and pads during your period.

After years of pads, you resent having to wear *diapers* once a month. After a few false starts, ask your mom to buy you regular tampons. Without asking any questions, she buys them. Your mom has seen the red and purple polka-dot thongs poking out of the laundry piles. You insert a teenage and size-appropriate tampon for the first time. It's got a pretty blue applicator, and it glides in like Disney on Ice. Once the main bit is in, it isn't clear where the tampon string goes. Carefully tuck the tampon string into your thong. Pee on many, many tampon strings. Flush a couple of tampons despite signs everywhere saying not to do that because you're sixteen and *rebellious*. Force yourself to ask your mom for birth control. Say it's for period cramps as you stare at your muddy shoes. Mom gets you birth control. She knows it's not for period cramps. Your mom is way cooler than you realize.

After two months on birth control, you're popping out of all of your bras. Your mom notices and takes you bra shopping and lets you pick out whatever you want. You know that "whatever you want" is code for boring and beige. You don't ask to try on the black lacy push-up, but as your mom stands in the checkout lane, you admire it from afar. You've seen your mom's bras. None of them are lacy or black.

Go to college and start buying your own sexy bras and period products with your *stipend*, a.k.a. college allowance, from your grandparents. Switch to all-cotton organic tampons. Feel like you're saving the world. Become a vegetarian. The week before Thanksgiving, start eating vegan like the cute guy in your creative writing class. Feel like an even better person. Your mom makes you dairy-free tofurkey without a fuss, and in turn, you say you're thankful for the environmentalist movement. Switch back to being a vegetarian when you find out the cute vegan guy is actually an asshole. There are better ways to be a good person. Learn about menstrual cups from your favorite yoga influencer. Buy a menstrual cup but then panic and leave it in the back of your desk drawer with a single purple sharpie to keep it company. Have sex during your period for the first time on an XL twin mattress. Feel like an *adult*.

Graduate college and get your first job. Receive your first paycheck. It's a lot less money than you expected. Learn about taxes. Switch from all-cotton organic tampons to whatever generic is cheapest. Screw environmentalism. In order to save even more money, fish out the menstrual cup from a dusty box in your closet and actually try it. Have sex with the cup in by accident; nothing bad happens. In April, ask your mom to file your tax return. She gets you $179.12 back from the Federal government. Donate $20 to the Sierra Club Foundation and spend the rest on a new pair of cherry red pumps.

Take baby steps toward becoming a more mature person. Schedule dental and physical appointments. Picture the rainforest being hacked away by loggers as a dental hygienist scrapes at your teeth with a metal instrument. At your physical, type notes on your phone as the doctor informs you on the importance of annual check-ins and how you need to see a gynecologist for a cervical cancer screening. Apparently, all women are supposed to get screened annually starting at twenty-one. Schedule a gynecology exam and feel proud of this follow-up. Three years late is better than never. Plus, it's taken you a while to understand how insurance works. You still don't really understand how insurance works, but at least now you know no one else understands it either. Go in for the gynecologist screening and walk out with an IUD and really bad cramps. The cramps go away in a day. Your period disappears a month later. The absence is new and strange. Splurge on new silky white underwear. You now finally own beautiful lingerie without having to worry about bloodstains. Wish you'd gotten the IUD sooner.

Read articles about how women were never supposed to menstruate monthly. Tell friends about how women spend the equivalent of ten years of their lives on their periods. You're enlightened, and your friends should be too. Tell your mom how she should be on birth control. Your mom chuckles and asks how your job is going and if you're seeing anyone. Mutter under your breath that your mom "doesn't really get it." The house is freezing cold. When you say you're going to change the temperature, your mom shakes her head no and offers you a wool sweater. Apparently, your mother likes living in a frozen tundra. She's been acting strange the last couple of months, but don't waste your time thinking about it.

Meet the first guy you actually see a future with. There's something about the crinkle around his mouth and the gruff of his voice, which makes you weak in the knees. Don't tell him you love him. You may be a feminist, but there's no point in scaring a good man away. Wait until he says it first in his soft, gravel voice. Introduce him to your mom over dinner. That way, you can justify drinking heavily through the experience. Take a tipsy catnap on the couch while your mom and this man spend hours discussing art history. Move in with your now boyfriend. Argue about whose coffeemaker gets thrown away. Keep both coffeemakers on the tiny kitchen counter of what used to be his bachelor pad. Buy new baby blue pillows for the couch. Get your expiring IUD removed and switch to condoms and pads. You're in a long-term relationship now, and you stopped wearing thongs the minute he asked you to split rent.

Get married. Try to get pregnant and get your period anyway. Try again and again. Cry to your mother over the phone. Turns out mom is a great listener. Have a lot of sex but not a lot of fun. Wonder if this is what it's like to be a porn star. Finally, you're pregnant and swollen and miserable. Hurray. Your mom buys you the largest cotton underwear you've ever seen in your whole life. Cry from joy. It may be the hormones, but you're pretty sure this is the nicest gift anyone has ever gotten you. Ask your mom about her experience being pregnant. Really listen as she tells you in excruciating detail how horrible it was to be pregnant with you. Tell your mom you're sorry for how difficult a fetus you were. Tell your mom you're sorry for how you never talked to her while you were growing up. Thank your mom for everything she's done for you over the years. Cry from sorrow when you notice your cup of tea has gone cold. Only stop crying when your mom brings you a new cup of tea.

Give birth to beautiful twins. They may be beautiful, but they're also fussy. You didn't know babies would cry so much. The sound scratches at your ears and makes your heartbeat go wild. Invite your mom to move into the guest room for a little bit. Finally, get some sleep. Go back to the office with your nipples sore and leaking. At night, stare at the ceiling and thank God for your beautiful babies, your husband, and especially for your mom. Five months later, your mom moves out but continues to come over Monday through Friday to babysit. Your period returns and bleeds through your pre-pregnancy pads, ruining a pair of pants. You buy new jumbo pads and XL tampons. Your kids begin to grow up in front of you. They walk, and talk, and dance like little miracles.

Wake up one day very hot and sticky. Cry often in the bathroom stall at work and after dropping the kids at Jiu-Jitsu. Miss your period. Get a pregnancy test. You're not pregnant. Go to the doctor. The doctor says you are perimenopausal. You're too young for menopause. Call your mom to vent. She listens sympathetically and says you'll save a lot of money on your heating bill this year. Laugh together. Spot blood on all of your underwear. Stop getting your period. Buy all-new all-cotton organic panties. Leave the XL period products in the back of your closet, just in case.

Live your life. Join the PTA and a book club. Shop at Costco with your mom, where you both buy comfort plus toilet paper in bulk. Decorate your house with seasonal throws and comic dishtowels. Your daughter tells you she has her first period. You hand her a super-absorbent jumbo pad. Warn her if she tries to shave her genitals she'll get ingrown hairs, and not to listen to any bullies. You think you're a *cool mom*, but don't worry. You're not.

CHAPTER TWO

GROWTH

———

"Girl's, it's time to talk about some changes your body is going to undergo in the near future," Mrs. Johnson stated, her words crisp and individually articulated. Mrs. Johnson was their sixth-grade Biology teacher. She wore silver-framed round eyeglasses and had posture so straight no one would ever guess she was only 5'4". All the girls, who'd previously been boisterously gossiping and giggling, went quiet. They huddled unmoving between the matte black laboratory tables, which smelled of Clorox and formaldehyde. All eyes in the room fixed on Mrs. Johnson.

The boys had all been ushered off by Mr. Marve, the gym teacher, to somewhere unknown, while Mrs. Johnson had led the fifty four-foot-tall female munchkins to the back of the science classroom. Usually, the only time the boys and girls weren't together was in the gym locker room. *Nobody here is taking off their clothes, so why are they separating us?* Elliott, a mousy brunette with large frizzy brown curls, had wondered. Not that she minded being away from the boys. The boys were smelly and loud, often bouncing off the walls and distracting Elliott from her thoughts.

Mrs. Johnson continued, "See, sometime in the next five years, you're all going to undergo something called puberty. When that happens, your body will change." Mrs. Johnson's gaze glided behind her spectacles from one girl to the next, locking eyes with each before moving on. While all the girls fixated on their teacher's face, Mrs. Johnson carried something resembling a small box of tissues in her hands.

"Some of you may already be experiencing these changes. Around the time these changes occur, you'll get your period, also called menstruation. A period is when you bleed out of your genitals approximately once a month."

An audible "Ew!" and another "Gross!" erupted from the crowd. Several jaws dropped. Elliott and many other girls remained unmoved either because they hadn't yet processed this news or because they'd already been educated about puberty. Elliott was in both camps. This was actually the second time she'd been told about periods, and she longed for more detailed information. *Can you pee while the blood is coming out? How much blood will come out? How quickly? Will I ever run out of blood? What will happen to my underwear? Do boys ever bleed out of their penises?*

"Shhh," said Mrs. Johnson with the force of a teacher who'd been dealing with sixth graders for over twenty years. "See this?" Mrs. Johnson held up the box with one hand, and with the other, she removed a white, plasticky object a little bigger than a deck of cards.

Elliott pushed the curls out of her face trying to get a better view. She was in the back edge of the throng.

"This is a pad." Tearing open the plastic cover, Mrs. Johnson unfurled the fluffy pad and tossed it into the crowd. "Here," she said. The rectangle seemed to float in the air for a second, falling in slow motion till it bounced off an immobile girl's face and sank to the floor. "Pick that up, please and pass it around," said Mrs. Johnson as she unwrapped and tossed another pad into the crowd.

The silence broke into giggles and murmurs. Now there were five pads hopping around the crowd like the beachballs at a concert Elliott had seen once on TV. No one seemed to want to hold onto them too long. Standing at the edge of the class, only one pad bounced near Elliott, and it was gone before she could really look at it. All she saw was the flapping of plastic coming off both sides of the fluffy middle. *What are those?* Elliott squinted as the pad flew away.

"If you get your period here at school, ask the nurse for a pad," Mrs. Johnson continued, but the focus of the group had shifted from her to the pads themselves. "The backing and wings will attach to your underwear."

There were squawks and squeaks. Not even Elliott was listening now. Mrs. Johnson continued, talking about marriage, babies, and disease, but all the girls noticed were the fluttering pads bouncing in the air.

Mrs. Johnson asked if anyone had any questions. Elliott didn't even consider raising her hand since talking to adults made her dizzy. With no questions to answer, Mrs. Johnson collected the pads, threw them in the trash, and led the girl group to the gymnasium where the boys were in the middle of a dodgeball game. Elliott hated dodgeball, but she was too deep in her own head to notice. She wandered onto the court with her arms swinging at her sides. Mrs. Johnson hadn't really answered any of her questions. Not that Elliott had voiced any questions, but she'd really been hoping Mrs. Johnson would give more details.

I wish someone had asked about the blood, Elliott thought as she stood in the back corner of the large rectangle painted on the shiny gym floor. Foam balls the size of pudgy piglets rolled by. One even flew through the air, scattering a group of gossiping girls nearby. One of the girls in the group, Abigail, gestured for Elliott to join them as they reformed. Elliott hesitantly did, standing in the unfamiliar circle.

"So, like I was saying, my older sister has her period, so I know *all* about it," said a girl named Ruth. "First, she got boobs, and then her period showed up like the next month! I'm in a training bra already, so I'm expecting mine like any day now." Ruth was flat as a board under her Abercrombie and Fitch tube top, but all the other girls nodded in agreement, including Elliott.

"Elliott, do you know anything about periods?" asked Abigail sweetly. "None of us had heard about it except Ruth and Yael since they have older sisters."

Elliott shook her head no, a white lie that made her blush.

"I want to know why they only told us girls," said Abigail, playing with the scrunchie on the end of her long braided hair.

"Duhhh, boys don't get periods Abigail!" said Ruth loudly. "If you have any period questions, you should like ask me."

"Why don't boys get periods?" asked Abigail.

"For the same reason they like don't get boobs," said Ruth, her head bobbing side to side. "They're boys!"

"Break it up, ladies! We're here to get exercise," Coach Marve yelled across the gymnasium, and the circle dissolved.

Elliott went back to her thoughts. *I wonder if boys don't get periods because they have penises... Penises. What a weird word.*

Elliott had learned the word penis a month earlier when her mom had decided it was time she learned where babies came from. They'd sat on her bed with its soft lavender comforter and talked for an hour—mostly Elliott's mom talking and Elliott listening. Elliott had learned the place where she peed was called a vagina, and men had a different pee part called a penis. Her mom told her not to let anyone touch her vagina until she was married, or she could get very sick. Elliott wasn't sure why anyone would ever want to touch where she peed, but she didn't dare ask her mother. Elliott's mom also told her she'd bleed a lot in her underwear once a month and not to worry about it. It was God's way of showing her she was special, that she could have babies someday when she was married.

Elliott had always been excited about someday having a baby, someone she could boss around, but knowing that involved someone touching her vagina and peeing blood, she was glad she wasn't going to have a baby anytime soon. The information from Mrs. Johnson had confirmed to Elliott vaginas were gross, and otherwise, she didn't want to think about it again.

***

When the summer rolled around a couple of months later, life was busy, and Elliott hadn't thought about periods or penises since that day in the gym. Sleepaway camp in Wyoming meant days filled with horseback riding, swimming, and crafting. It was beautiful at camp, full of sunny blue skies and fields full of flowers. Elliott and her new best friend Helen were constantly running between cabins, talking about their favorite horses Daisy and Buttercup, and mastering the sign language for *Cat's in the Cradle*.

Elliott had met Helen on the first day of camp when Helen walked up to her and declared, "I like your shirt. Pink is my favorite color! Are you going to ride horses this summer? I'm really excited about riding horses!"

That afternoon, Helen had asked Elliott to be her bunkmate. She'd also asked Elliott if she would mind if she, Helen, could have bottom bunk because she was deathly afraid of spiders, and spiders were more likely to attack the top bunk. Not that Helen wanted spiders to attack her new friend Elliott, but she thought Elliott would be better at defending herself. Helen had bright red hair, more freckles than they could count (they'd tried to one afternoon at lunch but had given up at thirty-seven), and she made Elliott feel warm and happy inside. Camp used the buddy system, so no camper was ever alone, and Elliott really appreciated always having Helen as her buddy.

Since Elliott had indeed signed up to ride horses, she and Helen had the same schedule and were always together. One day during arts and crafts, Elliott leaned in to carefully inspect the firetruck she was painting, and her large brown curls intermingled with the firetruck's cadmium red paint.

"You look good as a redhead," Helen laughed, her own red hair swept safely behind her ears.

"Not again..." Elliott mumbled. "My stupid hair just won't stay put." Elliott tried to assess how bad it was, but when she lifted her hands, she realized they also were covered in red paint. This wasn't the first time Elliott had distractedly gotten too close to her canvas, and every time, she wondered why the art cabin didn't have a mirror she could use to clean up. Thankfully, she had Helen to handle these situations.

"You're a mess," said Helen raising her hand. Without waiting for acknowledgment, Helen loudly asked, "Mr. Powski, can Elliott and I go to the bathroom?"

Mr. Powski nodded.

The two girls got up and skipped out of the art cabin and down the sunny path. As Elliott rubbed her hands together to try to get the paint off, it only spread further up her wrists, forming red gloves.

"Do you think they're going to give us apples for Daisy and Buttercup today?" asked Helen as she held open the door to the bathroom for Elliot. The bathroom was airy and smelled like real pine trees since the window above the door was always propped open to the outside. The yellow fluorescent light flickered slightly. Elliott had always found the dim insides of the metal stalls a bit eerie.

Elliott went to the sink, assessing how much paint was on her hands and her hair before turning on the faucet. Helen had already gone into a stall.

"I'm sure they will," said Elliott. *Silly Helen. They always give us apples for the horses*, she thought. Elliott smiled before returning to scrubbing her hands in the ice-cold camp water. For a minute, the only sound in the bathroom was the running faucet.

"Elliot, something's wrong," said Helen suddenly, her voice pitched higher than normal. Elliott could hear her gulping at the air.

"Helen!" said Elliott surprised at the volume of her own words.

"I'm bleeding! Do you think I'm going to die?" said Helen, the words tumbling out as though falling off a cliff.

"You're bleeding?" said Elliott trying to be calm, but her voice sounded too loud.

"It's my birthday next week. I'm going to miss my birthday and die at eleven!" wailed Helen.

"Helen, what happened?" said Elliott. Her words reverberated off the tiled floors and walls.

Helen didn't respond. All Elliott could hear were sobs. She could see Helen's freckled legs swaying through the gap at the bottom of the stall, Helen's feet not quite reaching the ground.

"Helen, where are you bleeding?" said Elliott. She was trying to be as level as possible, but her words came out loud and sharp. Her heart was pounding. *I can't handle this*, thought Elliott. *I can't help her. Helen might be dying, and I'm useless. Should I get Mr. Powski? But the buddy system! Should I call for help? Helen's better at screaming! She's better at everything. Should I ask her to call for help?* Elliott stood paralyzed. It felt like a rubber band was tightening around her throat.

"I don't know," Helen wept. "There's a lot of blood... in my underwear. It's probably cancer!"

Underwear? thought Elliott. *Underwear!* The rubber band was gone.

"Your underwear is full of blood?" said Elliot, each word enunciated. She'd never heard herself talk like this before, but Helen's life was too important to mince words. As Elliott stood staring at the stalls, she thought back to her mother and Mrs. Johnson and the way they'd looked in her eyes as they told her about peeing blood. Something about babies and the nurse. Flying bits of cotton dancing around the science lab.

Helen continued to sob.

"Helen, have you gotten your period before?" said Elliot, her voice smoother but still loud enough to bounce around the bathroom.

"My what?" Helen gulped between shallow breaths.

"Did they tell you at your school about your period? When you bleed once a month from your vagina?" said Elliott.

"Maybe?" sniffled Helen. "What's a vagina?"

"Where you pee from. Or something around there. You're not supposed to let anyone touch it. When you become an adult, it pees blood once a month." Elliott wrung her hands as she spoke and stared at the dull gray stall door behind which Helen sat. She tried to figure out what to say next.

"So... it's not cancer? It's a period? Are you sure?" said Helen, her voice cracking.

"I think so," said Elliott, squeezing her hands together. "I haven't gotten mine yet, but my mom told me it's God's way of telling you you're going to have babies someday. That you're special and healthy."

"Oh. Okay," said Helen pausing between her words. "I thought... because my uncle had cancer. He coughed blood before he died. But. This isn't cancer? Good. Good."

Elliott waited for a moment, unsure of what to tell Helen. She tried to remember what Mrs. Johnson had taught them. "At my school, they said you should go to the nurse, and she'd give you something. You wanna go together?"

"Uhh," said Helen and then went quiet.

Elliott, bouncing in place, began wracking her brain for the details. "She'll give you this thing to put in your under-wear—like a diaper for the blood," said Elliott.

"A diaper?"

"Yeah," said Elliott loudly, then bit her lip.

"Um, I think I need some time to sit," said Helen.

"Okay," said Elliott. A minute of painful silence passed, then Elliott could hear Helen pulling at the toilet paper roll. A cloud outside blew away, and several rays of sun began to shine into the bathroom from the open window above the door.

Elliott slowly turned back to the sink. She'd left the fau-cet on, and the water was gently gushing. She turned it off, then looked up in the mirror, where she saw the red paint still in her brown curls. Turning the sink back on, Elliott wet her hands before nervously combing the painted hair between her fingers. The bathroom was quiet other than the tinkling water.

It took a couple of minutes, but Elliott was able to get all the red paint out. She turned off the faucet and turned around. Beneath the stall door, Helen's legs hung unmoved. Elliott was unsure what to say or to do, but she wanted to say something. She couldn't just stand there, useless.

"I'm here for you, Helen. You're my best friend," said Elliott slowly. "You're going to be okay."

"I'm ready to go to the nurse now," said Helen after a moment. With the rustle of pants and the click of the metal door lock, Helen exited the stall, her eyes and nose a bit redder than before. "Thanks, Elliot."

Elliott nodded.

Helen washed her hands. As they turned to leave, Elliott hooked Helen's arm.

"It's pretty cool, you know," said Elliott. "I wish I had my period." She smiled, and Helen giggled softly.

"There's so much blood, Elliot. I stuffed my underwear with toilet paper," said Helen.

"Good thing I'm not a vampire then. You'd be irresistible," said Elliott. They both giggled as they walked into the sunshine. All the flowers seemed more colorful than before, and trees swayed in the gentle breeze. "We need to tell Mr. Powksi we're going to the nurse."

"Yeah, okay." Helen nodded as they walked back toward the art room.

"So I've always wanted to know," said Elliott, "how much blood and how fast is it coming out? You don't have to answer now, obviously."

"Buckets," said Helen wide-eyed.

Elliott looked at her friend dubiously.

"Okay, maybe not buckets, but it definitely ruined my favorite pair of purple underwear. It's like I poured a bottle of ketchup all over them. My mom won't even let me eat ketchup because she says there's too much sugar in it. And it's coming out like that leaky pipe outside of our cabin. Slow but drippy and super gross. Super super gross." Helen was beginning to sound like herself again, distracted and full of energy.

"Good to know," said Elliott, smiling as they approached the door to the art room arm-in-arm. "I have a couple more questions, but first, how about you wait here while I tell Mr. Powski we're going to the nurse?"

Helen nodded. A dark stain had begun to form at her crotch.

"Be back in a minute." Elliott entered the art room and walked right up to Mr. Powski, who looked at her curiously.

"Mr. Powski, Helen got her first period, so I'm going to take her to the nurse for a pad and then probably to our cabin to change. I wanted to let you know, so you weren't worried."

Mr. Powski grimaced mildly, nodded, and agreed.

Elliott went and rejoined her friend and held Helen's hand, leading the way to the nurse.

"You know you're my guardian angel," said Helen gripping Elliott's hand tightly. "I mean, you already were because of the whole spider slayer thing, and now you're even cooler."

"I haven't actually slain any spiders," said Elliott.

"Yeah, but you would for me. You even talked to Mr. Powski just now, and he's worth like at least a dozen spiders. You're the best friend I've ever had."

As the two friends walked down the path hand-in-hand, Elliott knew everything would be okay. For Helen, she would happily slay a dozen spiders, and if she was capable of that, Elliott realized she was capable of anything.

CHAPTER THREE

INTERSTATE 666

———

Zara's ninth birthday had been yesterday, September first. They'd celebrated with an amazing tres leches cake, Zara's favorite. The family had spent the day at the beach, energetically playing Marco Polo and Monkey in the Middle. During the busy day, Lola hadn't had a chance to talk to her little sister Zara privately. Today, Lola knew the perfect time to warn Zara of the impending changes to her young feminine body.

"Mama, can Zara and I go play outside?" said Lola. The two brunette girls were sitting with their mother at the round kitchen table, having just finished lunch. The three figures resembled Russian nesting dolls, similar but one smaller than the next.

"You know the rules. Plates in the dishwasher, and then you can go," said their mother Jane, barely glancing up from her sudoku puzzle.

Lola and Zara cleared their plates into the compost bin and placed them in the cavernous dishwasher. Lola, calling her sister to come with her, headed to the backdoor.

"I need to get Isabelle!" said Zara as she ran from the kitchen. Isabelle was Zara's blonde, gray-eyed American Girl doll.

"Hurry up!" said Lola as she went out the sliding door, squinting at the sunny grass.

Zara rushed outside, clutching Isabelle.

"Are you going to make me dribble again? Isabelle and I would rather watch you practice." Zara looked up with dread at the mountainous basketball hoop.

"No," Lola said, "today we're going to talk."

For the past month, Lola had been forcefully training Zara to be a basketball star. The training consisted of Lola repeatedly launching the basketball at Zara's face, followed by Zara dribbling once and throwing the ball about a foot in the air, not even close to the net. After maybe two dozen failed layup attempts, the ball would inevitably land on Zara's head, and Lola would begrudgingly let a huffing Zara take a break from practice. At her sister's shrugging acceptance, Zara would run away from the basketball that came up to her knees and sit in the shade to play with her doll.

"Okay," said Zara, her eyes narrowing. She stood frozen like a skeptical deer in headlights.

"Come sit," said Lola.

They sat on the prickly grass and, with Isabelle, they made a triangle. Zara had carefully placed her doll sitting upright, and she held its small hand in her not much larger palm. The breeze was fragrant with blooming flowers from the garden's Golden Apple tree, and nearby pale pink roses peaked out of a bush.

"Zara, I need to tell you something important. Something nobody else is gonna tell you until your twelve, not even mama, but by then, it'll be too late. You listen, okay?" said Lola. Zara nodded. The air was electric, fluttering the leaves on nearby trees with soft secret whispers.

"In the next two years, your body is going to do something called men-straight," said Lola. "It's part of being a grown-up, and it'll happen sometime soon. For me, it happened right when I was nine at Camp Waterlily. I thought I had pooped my favorite pants, but it was actually blood. See, when you men-straight blood comes out of from where you pee, and sometimes, it's brown like poop. Also, it's not the same hole as where you pee, but right next to it, I think. If you have poop stains in the front of your underwear, you're probably men-straighting."

Zara scrunched up her face. The tall grass blew around the pair, scratching at their exposed legs.

"I know it's terrible," continued Lola, "but it also means you're a woman, and being a woman is important. Women get to wear nail polish and makeup and have cellphones." She paused for emphasis. "Do you have any questions?"

Zara slowly shook her head as the sun bristled her back and caused her to itch. "Can I play with Isabelle now?" Zara asked, looking down at her doll. The doll's blank gray eyes looked off into the distance.

"Yes. We can take today off from basketball if you promise when you men-straight you'll tell me," said Lola. "I'm your sister, and I'm here to guide you. No one else is going to warn you about the front poop stains. They didn't warn me, and I want to make sure at least you know what's coming. So you promise you'll tell me?"

"Okay," said Zara. A cardinal with an aggressive red mohawk landed nearby. Its claws gripped an apple tree branch.

"Say you promise," said Lola.

"I promise," said Zara and interlocked her pinky finger with Lola's in a solemn swear.

The nearby cardinal was now chirping like a high-pitched car horn.

"No crossies count," said Lola. She nodded at Zara and then let go.

Zara immediately got up and took a couple of skips away before sitting back down in the shade to talk with her doll.

"I'm so glad she didn't make us play basketball today, Isabelle," said Zara to the doll. "I hate basketball!" Zara smoothed the front of Isabelle's dress. "Do you men-straight? No? Me neither." Zara continued talking as Lola watched from across the lawn. The cardinal hopped off the nearby tree and swiftly flew away.

***

Zara turned ten and then eleven without incident. On her twelfth birthday, when Zara still hadn't come to her with her period, Lola confronted her. But there was nothing to tell. Zara told Lola she wasn't yet menstruating.

Lola, now fifteen, had thought something was wrong. Lola felt she'd waited long enough to raise the issue. It was time to address her concerns to their mother.

Jane was at the quartz kitchen island when Lola approached her. Vegetables cluttered the counter, and Jane was chopping some tomatoes on a worn wooden board.

"Mama, I'm worried about Zara," said Lola.

Jane looked up at her daughter, who stood across the large island from her. The air was fragrant and spicy, and Lola's nostrils fluttered at the scents.

"Is this about Zara not wanting a birthday party? Lola, your sister's not like you. She's shy," said Jane. Sunshine smoldered through the window across the island between mother and daughter.

"No, mama, I already talked with Zara about that. This is something I need to talk with *you* about. I'm worried that Zara hasn't gotten her period."

"Hmmm," Jane cooed, tilting her head slightly as she continued to dice tomatoes, their transparent juices oozing off the wooden cutting board and forming a pool of red on the glimmering white countertop. Jane kept cutting, ignoring the growing mess.

"Zara is twelve now," said Lola. "Twelve, and she hasn't gotten her period. What if something's wrong with her? You need to do something, Mama." Lola stared at her mother, willing her to understand the significance of the concern.

Jane looked up, and the chopping briefly stopped. "Lola, there is nothing wrong with your sister."

"But Mama, I got my period right at nine!" exclaimed Lola. "You told me you got your period at nine. I talked to Marisol about this, and she got her period at nine." Marisol was Lola and Zara's first cousin, right between them in age. "Zara is twelve now. Twelve! She's years behind." Lola paused, glaring at Jane. "What if you're ignoring something big here?"

"It's great that you care, Lola, but Zara is fine. Many girls get their periods when they're twelve," said Jane as she resumed chopping, the knife thudding decisively against the cutting board.

"Not in this family," said Lola with gumption. She watched her mother like a hawk as Jane continued to dice. The juices were everywhere now.

"How about this," said Jane, "I'll ask the doctor about it at Zara's next physical. In the meantime, you stop worrying about your sister and focus on yourself. We both know you've got basketball tryouts next week." Jane grabbed another swollen tomato to dice.

"Fine. But don't say I didn't warn you," said Lola. With that, Lola swiftly turned around and stormed out of the kitchen without looking back.

Lola was fuming, talking to herself. "First, she never warns me about my period, and I'm left blindsided. Now, she doesn't even care that something might be wrong with Zara!" Lola slammed the front door as she exited the house. "What's the point in parents having power if they're not going to do anything?"

***

Over a year later, Lola's friend was telling an embarrassing story about her sister using tampons incorrectly (only inserting them halfway, like a corked bottle) when Lola thought about her own sister Zara. She didn't want Zara to be embarrassed or have issues, and there was a real problem. Zara still didn't have her period. Yes, their mother had refused to do anything last year, but now Lola was going to take the situation into her own hands. She would force Jane to see the light.

After her monthly check-in with Zara, who confirmed she still wasn't menstruating, Lola confronted their mother. Jane responded she hadn't been there to ask at the doctor's appointment last year, but she remembered girls' father Carlos saying the doctor thought Zara was healthy. In fact, Jane had just scheduled Zara's next doctor's visit, and she told an indefatigable Lola that she would be sure to ask about Zara's late menstruation then.

Unsatisfied, Lola asked if she could come to the appointment. That way, she could ensure it was checked correctly. Jane agreed but added that Lola would need Zara's permission to come along. Lola added the appointment to her calendar.

***

The day before the appointment came, Lola cornered Zara in the tight lilac bathroom they shared. Zara was brushing her teeth.

"Zara, I *need* to come to the doctor's with you tomorrow. Mama said I had to ask your permission, so can I come?"

Zara, now a small thirteen-year-old, spit out her bubblegum toothpaste. She was wearing her old pajamas with pants that were too short and a top that exposed her protruding belly button. Jane had tried to donate the ensemble to charity, but Zara had snuck them out of the donation pile and back into her drawer.

"I guess. Is something wrong?" said Zara, reaching for a butterfly embossed Dixie cup to rinse her mouth. Her hair was wet and smelled like a halo of citrus shampoo.

"Yeah, you don't have your period," said Lola, "unless something's changed in the last month and you haven't told me yet?"

Zara spit out the water in her mouth and dully shook her head no.

"Okay," said Lola. "Well, I want to make sure you're healthy. Someone needs to check."

"You don't think Mom has the doctor's appointment covered?" said Zara tentatively, unraveling the empty Dixie cup in her hand to a swirl of paper.

"Mom dropped the ball last year on asking the doctor about your period, and she didn't even warn me before I got mine," said Lola, placing her hand on her sister's cold shoulder. "Would you have preferred that? No one warning you? Not having an emergency pad when it finally happens so you bleed all over your favorite pair of overalls? Because you know that's what happened to me. Not only did I miss a day of camp, but someone started a rumor that I peed myself. I got called *pee pants* the rest of the summer! You want to be called pee pants?"

"No, I guess not," said Zara, tossing the now crumpled cup. "I need to floss." Zara lifted her elbow slightly, within centimeters of her sister's chest, to show there was no room for both of them in the bathroom during this next step.

Lola nodded and said, "I'll be there tomorrow. Love you, sissy!"

***

"How are we all doing today?" asked Doctor Rabinovitz. The small office was cramped as Lola, Zara, and Jane were all standing holding their big winter puffy coats. It was January and freezing outside. The fluorescent lighting above buzzed annoyingly like the cicadas of midsummer.

"Good," Lola said cheerily.

"Lola, didn't I see you last week?" asked Doctor Rabinovitz. She wore a stethoscope around her neck like a garden snake, and her monochrome dyed brown hair matched her eyes.

Before Lola could answer, Jane cut her off, "Today's appointment is for Zara."

"Ah, hello, Zara, how are you doing today?" said Doctor Rabinovitz to Zara, who stood close to her mother with almost her entire body hidden by her large coat.

"Good," Zara mumbled.

"Much quieter than your sister, aren't you?" said Doctor Rabinovitz, an older woman with an affable smile the girls had seen many times since they were born. "Up on the table then. Your height and weight look healthy, though decidedly on the smaller side." Doctor Rabinovitz looked down at the nurse's notes. "Up to date on vaccinations. I have a couple of questions for you, a couple of things I need to check, any questions you have, and then you're on your way. Not too scary, is it?" The doctor paused, putting the chart down and looking at Zara. "I can't believe you're already thirteen! Fun age, isn't it? Have you begun menstruating?"

"No," said Zara, examining the tattered ends of her pink shoelaces.

"I got mine at nine, and so did our cousin and Mama," cut in Lola.

"Ah, I see." Doctor Rabinovitz turned to Lola. "But your sister is going to take a bit longer. That's normal."

"Are you sure there's nothing wrong with her?" said Lola without pause. "Can you check her for an imperforate hymen? Those can be dangerous. I've ruled out diabetes and malnutrition, though Zara is pretty thin. Or could she be intersex? Half of intersex people don't have a period." Lola recited this recently memorized monologue quickly, ignoring the wide eyes of her mother and Zara's downturned face.

"Lola, stop it! What are they teaching you in health?" said Jane, glaring at Lola.

Zara's face had contorted like a Salvador Dali clock, melting into a gaping mouthed look of terror.

"I googled reasons for not getting a period, and Marisol taught me about intersex because she has an intersex friend," said Lola confidently. "Zara has the right to her own health information. It's part of HIPAA!"

"Lola!" barked Jane, her face flush with embarrassment.

"You're not doing enough, Mama! Zara deserves to know if something's wrong. You never warned me before I got my period or explained discharge or labia growth. I had to figure out absolutely everything on my own. Now, something's actually wrong with Zara's vagina, and I won't abandon her!"

Shocked silence followed Lola's explosion. Lola stood tall, her chin jutting into the air as if waiting to be challenged. Jane was red-faced in shock. Zara had buried her face into her coat. Doctor Rabinovitz, eyes a bit enlarged, looked from face to face as if they were all puzzle pieces.

Then the silence was broken. Doctor Rabinovitz spoke with a level voice, "Lola, your sister is healthy, and no one is abandoning her. I've been treating you both for a very long time, and I can confidently say Zara does not have any health issues, and she is not intersex. If she did have any health challenges, I would've talked to Jane about them since Zara is a minor. Lola, you're a bright young cookie, but you're wound up, and that is not helping your sister. The best thing you can do is talk with your mother one-on-one about your experience and give Zara some space. Zara will get her period when she goes through puberty. In the meantime, Lola, you should be careful with diagnosing yourself or others medically. It's a very slippery slope."

The room fell quiet yet again, except for the light, which continued to buzz overhead.

"Doctor Rabinovitz, am I broken? Please tell me," whispered Zara shielded behind her coat. Zara had her hands wrapped around her own neck like a noose. "I know I'm four years late." As Zara spoke, the room seemed to shrink, the feverishly bright posters of food garishly staring down at Lola.

"Zara! No, you're a very beautiful, healthy young woman," the doctor said with warmth, leaning over to Zara. " Not getting your period by thirteen doesn't mean you're broken! Like I said, you'll get your period when it's your time for puberty. You've got years before I'd be concerned. You should not be worried. Many healthy girls get their period when they're sixteen."

"Sixteen!" cried Lola, jolting forward.

"Shhhh!" hushed Jane aggressively, pulling at Lola's arm. Lola pulled her arm away from her mother, but neither Doctor Rabinovitz nor Zara looked over.

Doctor Rabinovitz continued, "Yes, sixteen. You shouldn't worry, Zara. You're going to be just fine." The doctor's smooth hand now rested on Zara's shoulder, radiating tranquility. "If your period hasn't come four years from now, when you're seventeen, I can double-check if your uterus has spontaneously disappeared, but until then, you'll have to make do with being a healthy thirteen-year-old girl who will get her period when it's her time, no matter how much others try and rush it." With that, the doctor winked at Zara.

Zara's rigid body relaxed, almost as if she had liquified into a pool on the exam table. The rest of the appointment was uneventful. Lola was silent. It felt like time was on fast-forward, and soon Jane was apologizing and thanking Doctor Rabinovitz as they got up to leave.

After the doctor's visit, Lola simmered in the car on the ride home, and Zara was equally quiet. When Jane offered to get Zara frozen yogurt, both girls shook their heads, "No."

"Not for you, Lola," Jane said. "We need to talk."

"Whatever," Lola responded. When they got home, Lola headed to her bedroom. Thankfully Jane didn't follow her. Lola knew her mother wasn't happy, but in spite of the visit's conclusion, Lola didn't regret her choice to speak up.

"So that was disappointing," Lola said to her empty bedroom. She went and stretched across her bed. "I think Doctor Rabinovitz should have taken my concern more seriously."

Zara appeared in the doorway of Lola's room, the bright hallway making her slender figure look taller in its shadow. "Lola, I need to say something, and I need you to listen."

"Okay," said Lola, watching the ceiling fan circle overhead.

"I need you to stop meddling in my period life. Like Doctor Rabinovitz said, you need to give me space."

Lola felt the bedspread bristle under her hands. "I was only trying to help today," said Lola, the confidence in her voice unwavering, "I'm your sister and apparently the only one who's looking out for you."

Zara spoke from her position in the doorway. "But you didn't help. You made me feel like a wacko broken person. Why do you keep rubbing it in my face that I'm behind? Why do you ask me every month if I've gotten my period? Why do you keep telling me that there's something wrong when the doctor says I'm fine?" Lola could see Zara shaking as she spoke.

"I'm being careful. I thought we should get a doctor's opinion," said Lola, still staring back up at the fan.

"Lola, I heard what you said about being abandoned. That sucks, but it also sucks to have an older sister smother you. I will never forget today. It was awful, and you didn't need to do that to me. From now on, I want you to leave me alone. I'd rather be abandoned than have you make me feel this scared and hopeless."

Lola's face began to burn like a fresh tomato in the sun. Lola had never imagined how this situation would make her sister feel less-than. Lola had only wanted Zara to be prepared and supported like she hadn't been.

"I was helping," said Lola, "I did research!"

"But you're not helping. You're making things terrible. Every time you involve yourself, I'm left anxious. I didn't swim in the ocean for years because I thought my scent would attract sharks!"

"I didn't tell you that!" said Lola defiantly.

"No, you just said I would start randomly bleeding any day now, and I needed to prepare. Well, I prepared! For as long as I can remember, I've taken an emergency pad with me everywhere I've gone. I stopped swimming in the ocean. I go to the bathroom way more than I have to pee so I can check for blood. I've spent four years afraid of nothing because of you." The words were stinging and full of pain.

"I was trying to protect you," said Lola. She was only a few feet away on the bed, but the distance felt vast. Overhead, the fan's blades circled like crows waiting to pick apart a carcass.

"Well, you did a terrible job," said Zara, who remained in the doorway.

"I'm sorry," said Lola. The apology seemed to bounce out the bedroom, past Zara, and into the quiet hallway. Zara remained silent.

"I'm so sorry," said Lola again. "I only wanted you to be prepared and healthy."

"Why do you always imply that I'm unhealthy? What makes me unhealthy, not being like you?"

"No, Zara, no, this isn't about me! I…"

"It's always been about you!" said Zara, her voice breaking.

Lola could see her sister's eyes glistening. Getting up, Lola crossed the distance between them, walking through the shag rug toward her sister in the doorway. Lifting her arms gently, Lola wrapped them around Zara, embracing her in a hug that smelled of vanilla lotion. Zara didn't hug her back. Lola could feel Zara's frenetic breathing.

"I love you, sissy. I love you so much," said Lola, muffled by the hug she was giving. "And I'm sorry. I overcorrected because no one ever helped me. I'm sorry I made this about me."

"And you should talk to Mama about that, but stop taking it out on me." Lola, still trapping Zara in an embrace, shook heavily between the unsteady words.

"Okay," said Lola, "I'll talk to Mama. About me this time. I'm so sorry. I love you so much." They stood there for a while, intertwined.

Eventually, Zara reached one arm around Lola, half-heartedly returning her hug, and then pulled free of the engulfing embrace. "I'm gonna go," said Zara, "but I do love you too, maniac."

Lola gave her a weak smile. Zara turned with her shoulders drooped in exhaustion and walked away.

CHAPTER FOUR

SOS

———

When Ted knocked on Nadine's door for the dance, he looked perfect. His hair was neatly combed, the black tux looked tailored, and his shoes shined.

"Oh, look how handsome, straight out of a catalog!" Nadine's mother fawned. Nadine's father put down *The Economist* magazine he'd been reading, stood up from his austere leather chair to shake Ted's. Even the Virgin Mary seemed to smile at Ted from an oil painting on the wall.

"Thank you, ma'am and sir. Nadine, you look beautiful," said Ted gallantly.

Nadine was wearing a tight one-shoulder pale pink dress adorned with sparkling rhinestones. She carried an equally bedazzled clutch which was just large enough for her phone, lipstick, and breath strips. Her shoes, a full two inches, were the tallest her mother would allow, but Ted still towered over her.

"Thank you." Nadine smiled while eyeing Ted up and down. *He looks edible.*

Soon they were in the limo with Ted's soccer friends. Inside, neon lights in the ceiling illuminated the clean-shaven players grouped in the front half of the limo and their dolled-up dates packed tightly in the back. One of the dates had put on too much of her mother's perfume, and the smell was like bathing in rotting flowers. Though no one commented, Nadine wasn't the only one mouth breathing to avoid the scent.

Nadine had hoped there'd be alcohol in the limo. Cool kids drank alcohol and then had sex. The sight of the limo's empty built-in bar, its hammered metal surface reflecting the lights above, didn't weigh too heavily on Nadine's hope. If there was alcohol, she knew it would be hidden. Hillary, Nadine's best friend, had gone to homecoming last year with a group that had surreptitiously passed around alcohol-laced sodas. But, after being handed a water bottle full of only water, Nadine was disappointed to discover the soccer team's limo was dry that night. Something about soccer being too important to risk drinking before a school event. Not that they ever drank. Nadine had been hanging out with them for months, and despite *being cool*, they were always sober and celibate. Thankfully this mild letdown only momentarily phased Nadine. She was going to homecoming with Ted and his candy lips, and they were going to have sex with or without alcohol, and that's all that mattered.

While Ted joked around with his pack, Nadine attempted conversation with the other girls. Hillary's current boyfriend Jerome was in Acapella, not soccer or any other sport, so they were in a different limousine. Jerome was not what Nadine expected when Hillary first mentioned having a new boy toy. Before Jerome, Hillary had gone through a string of boyfriends she dumped like day-old pastries. Unlike her previous companions, Jerome wasn't muscularly sculpted or as tall as a redwood, plus he was in a nerdy singing group, but Hillary had been dating him for a few months now and seemed genuinely happy with her choice.

Nadine pictured Hillary drinking vodka from a plastic water bottle as Jerome emphatically harmonized with the rest of the limo to "The Story of Tonight" from the musical *Hamilton*. Hillary said the whole troupe was obsessed with the musical. Instead, Nadine was stuck with the soccer heads, a wealthy group of girls she and Hillary called the "brat pack," and a few random females Nadine had never met before. *They probably go to the public school*, thought Nadine about the randoms, *lucky, they get to go to school with boys*. While the brat pack were perfectly nice to Nadine, she and the other randoms mostly listened as they talked to one another. *This is going to be the best night of my life*, thought Nadine as one of the pack rattled on about how long it had taken the hairdresser to curl her extensions.

The only thing that mattered to Nadine was that tonight was special, and it was going to be. For starters, Ted's Catholic boys school was loaded. After the homecoming dance, they had a school-sponsored after-party on a yacht. Apparently, the boys' parents paid for the boat to prevent DUI fatalities, or even worse, teenage pregnancy. *A night of firsts! First homecoming dance, first time on a yacht, and first time having sex!*

Nadine stared longingly at Ted as he chatted up his friends. Ted Pagerman was a dirty blond, blue-eyed, all-American male that Nadine had claimed as her boyfriend a couple of months prior. They'd all been sitting outside in the smoke of a campfire, roasting marshmallows and talking about upcoming junior year class schedules. Nadine had beelined to Ted, who was sitting on a plastic folding chair like Zeus on a throne, and coyly asked him if his lap was available.

When he nodded, she had sat down sideways, turned her torso toward him, and pressed herself against his chest. They had kissed. All the other boys had hooted and hollered, but Nadine didn't mind. Ever since that night, they'd been an item. It was like living in a dream or dating a famous actor.

When the limo arrived at the high school gym for the dance, Ted sat them at a table with the soccer bros nowhere near Hillary and Jerome. Nadine had expected this and tried not to be disappointed. The tablecloths were thin plastic, and Nadine could see the tables underneath lit by the incessantly pulsating dance lights. *Is this DJ trying to give me a stroke?* Nadine settled into her seat, sandwiched between Ted and his friend Rodney. Rodney didn't have a date. Rodney had told Ted to tell Nadine to find him a date, but her friend, who'd initially said yes, canceled a week before the dance because her brother had lice, making Nadine look decidedly uncool. Now Rodney acted like Nadine wasn't even there, yelling to Ted like a foghorn over the throbbing music about the team's new offense. With her ear next to Rodney's mouth, Nadine thought she would go deaf.

Nadine was thankful when Ted got up to get drinks and took Rodney and Matteo, another teammate, with him. At least no one would be yelling now. Nadine evaluated her surroundings as she waited for Ted to come back and bring her a Diet Coke with lemon.

The gym was fine, not as grand as she had expected. The decorations were lackluster. There were a number of paper streamers and a few dozen black and gold balloons. While someone clearly had tried to make the gym look sophisticated, they had failed. It still looked like a high school gym.

Still waiting for Ted to return, Nadine watched the DJ, a kid with oily hair, spring up and down like a bobblehead to the frenzied beat of his music. On the dance floor, there were already some couples taking selfies and others bopping to the *rhythm*. Nadine inspected her manicure. Everyone except one canoodling couple had left her table. She wanted to go find Hillary, but Ted would be annoyed if he came back to the table and she wasn't there. Nadine didn't want to spoil this important night. Plus, Ted would bring her a drink. *No, I'll wait for Ted. He should be back any minute.*

Most of the night went like that. Nadine waited around while Ted hung out with Rodney or other soccer teammates. Ted took a break from sports to ask Nadine to dance, but they were quickly sent back to their table for dinner. Then, even the mediocre soggy chicken dinner was peppered with constant soccer talk. After a few hours, while Ted seemed totally consumed by the conversation at the table, Nadine snuck off to say hi to Hillary.

"They're going to round everyone up soon to shove you on the boat," said Hillary, unenthused. Hillary had been invited to homecoming last year, while Nadine had still been in a training bra. "I told my mom that Jerome and I are doing the boat, but once was enough for me. The dance was the fun part anyway."

"What are you going to do instead?" asked Nadine.

"You know, drive around." Hillary butted shoulders with Nadine, who could momentarily feel her friend's skin, hot from dancing. 'Driving' was code for fooling around in the back of Jerome's car. She partially wished she and Ted were doing the same. She had barely seen Ted tonight.

"I really like this one," Hillary continued. "You know he serenaded me in the limo in front of all the guys in his acapella group? Much better than the jocks I've dated, a real

sweetheart. His friends too, even if they are all into musicals."
Hillary rolled her eyes and smiled.

"That's nice," said Nadine, mentally comparing the girth
of Jerome's to Ted's arms. *I wonder if arm girth is correlated
with girth elsewhere...*

"Well, I got to go," said Hillary giving Nadine's arm a
squeeze. "Love you, babe!"

Then Hillary and Jerome were gone, and Nadine was left
looking for Ted again.

"Where have you been?" Ted asked when she finally found
him. He made a show of giving her a big smooch in front of
the circle of soccer pals.

"Just saying hi to Hillary," she responded. *Ted may be a
jock, but he's a sweetheart too. He cares about me.*

"Good," said Ted, frowning. He placed his arm firmly
around her waist. "So, our next game..."

Ted resumed talking soccer strategy with Rodney, and
it all sounded like buzzwords to Nadine. The group smelled
of men's deodorant and swimming pools of aftershave. Rodney, as always, loudly asserted his point of view. More than
one fleck of spit flew from Rodney's mouth and landed on
Nadine's arm and face. She tried to back away from the spit
source as they headed to the line for busses to the boat, but
Ted's muscular arm placed her right back in Rodney's range.

As soon as they were on the ship, Nadine finally excused
herself to go to the ladies' room. She searched for and found
one of the few bathrooms available on the boat. Despite it
being 11 p.m., the bathroom was bright, the mirror rimmed
with lights, and the floor sparkled aqua. This bathroom alone
had more class than the entire gymnasium from the dance.
Nadine patted her face with a napkin, careful not to smudge
her makeup.

I can't believe Hillary didn't want to come on the boat, thought Nadine as she unzipped the dress from under her arm. *She's going to be so jealous of our photos. This place is stunning! Clearly, this is going to be even better than the dance. Ted and I just need to find a quiet corner to heat things up. Tonight will be perfect.* The pale pink dress dropped to the ground and underneath Nadine was naked. The elastic dress had shown underwear lines, and Nadine's mom wouldn't let her wear thongs. Nadine had thought about buying a thong for the evening, but since her mom did the laundry, she figured it was risky. Instead, Nadine had gone commando.

Nadine was about to flush the toilet when she noticed something odd about the toilet paper in the bowl. A dark streak in the floating soup of weak yellow. Nadine wiped again. Looking at the toilet paper, it was bright red.

Christ! thought Nadine. She opened her purse, looking for a period product she knew wasn't there. Nadine looked around the bathroom. It was sleek, everything made of glass and semi-transparent. Nowhere for a box of tampons to be tucked away.

Nadine balled up some toilet paper and put it between her thighs, pulling up and zipping her dress. After washing her hands, Nadine shuffled quickly out of the bathroom. The toilet paper ball rubbed between her legs.

Dear God, please don't let it fall down or leak. Also, God, please help me find a tampon. Amen, prayed Nadine.

Nadine looked for anyone she knew, hoping one of the brat pack would save her. It felt like a real-world version of "Where's Waldo," but with higher stakes. The boat was lit with hazy moonlight, full of contorted faces laughing in huddled packs. No one was recognizable.

"You disappeared again," said Ted, coming up beside Nadine as she attempted to scan the faces around her. "Everyone's been pairing up, so I was thinking we should find our own dark corner." Ted flashed his brilliant info-mercial-worthy smile, but Nadine was looking past him and barely noticed.

"Not right now, Ted. Have you seen any of the brat pack? Sorry, I mean any of the girls we shared a limo with?" said Nadine. Squirming teenagers packed the boat.

"Like I said, off with their boyfriends," said Ted. "You really want to go gossip instead of hanging out with me?" His voice was playful, like a cat toying with a mouse, but Nadine wasn't playing her usual role.

"No, I just have a situation I need to take care of," said Nadine, scanning the crowd.

"Whatever it is, I'm sure it can wait," said Ted confidently, reaching out for Nadine's hips.

"It really can't," said Nadine pulling away, "I'll see you soon." Nadine left Ted standing there as she shuffled away.

Finding one of the limo girls, Nadine asked her, "Do you have a tampon?"

"No," said the first girl she asked.

"Sorry," said the next.

Soon Nadine had given up on finding people she knew and was asking every female she passed. With their tiny clutches or no purse at all, none of them had a tampon.

Nadine could feel blood beginning to trickle down her inner thighs as the toilet paper continued to rub between her legs. The boat shook in the dark sea.

Finally, Nadine found someone who offered her a pad, commenting that she didn't use tampons because she was saving herself for marriage.

"Thank you, thank you! You're my savior!" Nadine practically cried, taking the pad. Shuffling back to the bathroom and unzipping her dress, she remembered she wasn't wearing any underwear. In her desperation to get a period product, she'd forgotten that pads needed underwear to stay in place.

Thankfully, the blood that had run between her thighs and smeared about as she shuffled hadn't yet touched her dress or gone past its hemline. Nadine quickly wiped the blood away with toilet paper and water. With that cleaned up, Nadine examined the pad. It had wings, bits of plastic sticking out from the sides with adhesive on the back. Removing the plastic backing of the adhesive wings, Nadine stuck them to her inner thighs. The pad hung like a hammock between her legs. Nadine took a step across the bathroom. The pad's adhesive was strong enough to hold as long as she took small steps, but only small steps.

This will have to do. She pulled her dress back on. The tight fabric now bulged at the groin, but that was the least of Nadine's worries. Still shuffling, this time the speed of molasses, Nadine went to go find somewhere to sit. *If I sit, it won't come undone*, thought Nadine. The blood flow was gaining momentum, and Nadine could now feel fluid oozing out of her vagina. *There goes any chance of losing my virginity tonight.*

Squeezing between the hordes, Nadine navigated to an empty table near the boat's buffet and situated herself. It smelled like the fryer at a McDonald's, and the tablecloth was askew and stained with ketchup. Checking her phone, Nadine had no notifications. She thought about texting Ted but decided he was better off hanging out with his buddies than taking care of her. If he was talking soccer, which he definitely was, maybe he wouldn't notice she was gone. If he did notice, he would surely text or call. Plus, she'd rather not explain to Ted what was happening. Nadine watched TikTok to kill time and hoped the boat dropped them off soon. It was around midnight now, so it probably wouldn't be too long.

Nadine's phone battery was on its last legs when Ted found her.

"Where have you been?" said Ted. He carried his jacket over one shoulder, and his white tuxedo shirt clung to his sweaty chest.

"Here," said Nadine. "I'm glad you found me; I was just about to text you. Want to sit and talk?"

"No, the team is all dancing on the deck. Let's go," said Ted. From her seat, Nadine could see some teens humping on the dimly lit dance floor.

"I can't dance," said Nadine, shuffling in her seat. She could feel the adhesive pucker as her legs moved. "Do you know when the boat docks?"

"Around six," said Ted.

"6 a.m.?" Nadine's voice raised an octave. The greasy buffet smell had permeated her hair and dress.

"Yeah, then we can go park behind the library like we talked about." Ted smiled knowingly.

"Oh, I actually can't tonight," said Nadine and watched as Ted's smile morphed into a scowl. *What do I tell him? This is so embarrassing.*

"Huh. Well, we've got another five hours, so why don't you come dance with me? I can't slow dance alone." Ted held out his hand in an old-fashioned gesture that looked almost robotic, like a cyborg. Nadine could taste the hot stress saliva building up in her mouth.

"I can't, Ted," said Nadine again, unsure of what to say and whether to tell him.

Ted stood across the table from her, looking down at Nadine in her chair. He lowered his hand and spoke in a deep voice. "First, you don't find Rodney a date, then you go missing half the night, and now you'd rather sit here alone than spend time with your boyfriend? Not to mention abandoning our post-dance plans. Come on, Nadine, you're making me look terrible. The other guys are saying you're wasting my time."

"They're what?" said Nadine flabbergasted. She'd never known the team to talk about anything but soccer, and now they were giving Ted relationship advice?

"I told them you're alright, but after the Rodney thing, you were yellow-carded. Hell, Rodney told me to break up with you. He thinks I can do better."

"I have my period," said Nadine. She could feel the boat rocking underneath as her chair gave an unsteady shudder. "I was gone trying to find a tampon for my period."

"Hold it in!" commanded Ted. "Instead, you go gallivanting around and then completely disappeared. You made it look like I came to homecoming stag. As if I couldn't get a date! There are over a dozen girls on this ship alone who would have killed to be here with me, and I asked you. Get it together, Nadine, and come dance with me and the team. Now."

Nadine sat there, fire beginning to build in her stomach. *Hold it in? Yellow-carded?* She looked up at Ted, her back straightening and her words loud and sharp. "I can't believe this. *You* were gone most of the night with your 'soccer buddies,'" Nadine did air quotes, "and you have the audacity to question where *I* was? I literally spent all of the dance waiting around for you and letting your friends spit in my face about defense strategy. That was until I got trapped in this hellhole of a boat, bleeding from my vagina. We were supposed to have sex tonight. Do you even know what a vagina is? I told you I'm dealing with my period, and you think I should hold it in? There is blood gushing from my vagina, Ted. Gushing. It's basic biology. I know you go to a Catholic all boys school, but are you seriously *that* ignorant?"

Ted's face was beat red, and Nadine could see his eyes dart around the room. Some of the couples nearby had stopped dancing, clearly listening to the conversation.

"I take you to my homecoming, and now you're making a scene? Calling me names? I think we're done here," said Ted. He stood firmly in place, holding his ground with his feet shoulder width apart.

"Are you breaking up with me?" said Nadine, her nostrils flared.

Nearby murmurs rumbled through the small crowd.

"I wasn't sure, but yeah, I think I am. I can do better."

"Fuck you."

"Rodney's right, you are a cunt," shouted Ted as he stormed away. The few people who'd been listening backed quickly toward the dancefloor, leaving Nadine isolated in her rage.

Nadine closed her eyes tight and tried to understand what had just happened. Nearby, a plate clattered to the floor. Opening her eyes, Nadine looked at her phone. *I need to conserve the battery. Otherwise, I won't be able to call for a ride home.* She and Ted were supposed to drop Rodney off at his house and then drive to the library to have sex, but that plan had gone up in smoke. She sent a quick text to Hillary:

don't text back

phone dying

ted and I are done!

ride back home from the boat would be appreciated

6am dock

Nadine turned off her phone and lay her head on the table to try and get some sleep. Maybe she could forget the night had ever happened. Maybe she could forget Ted had ever happened. As Nadine drifted off, her last thought was, *he was a shitty kisser anyway.*

***

Nadine was jarred awake by the boat docking. Her stomach and head ached. It took her a minute to process where she was and why everything smelled greasy. Then she remembered. *How am I going to get home?*

Her area of the boat had emptied, leaving the lingering scent of body odor and fried food. When Nadine got up, she felt the adhesive pulling at her thighs, the pad drooping between her legs. Leaving the enclosed cabin, the deck was bright with bleary-eyed teenagers crowding to exit the boat. Nadine spotted the soccer team toward the front, about to exit, their tall heads held above the rest of the crowd. She saw them leave. Ted's hair sparkled golden blond in the sun as he walked away, not once looking back at the boat for her.

It's not fair he's so beautiful, thought Nadine, *jerk.* She turned on her phone to find no notifications.

Nadine exited the boat, about to call her mom when she heard someone yell, "Nadine, over here!"

It was Hillary, leaning out the passenger side window of Jerome's white sedan, her hair a spectacular frizzy mess.

Knowing the pad might detach, Nadine stopped herself from running to the car and instead shuffled as quickly as she could toward her friend.

"You okay, babe?" said Hillary as Nadine got in the back-seat. "You're walking funny." The fabric seat was warm and fuzzy, uncomfortably rubbing Nadine's bare thighs. In the background, a song from the musical *Six* played softly out of the speakers, irritating Nadine's headache.

"Yeah, thanks for coming. Just get me home," said Nadine, staring at her ruined shoes covered in scuffs.

"Will do," said Hillary and started giving directions to Jerome.

Nadine stewed in her own misery in the backseat and watched as they drove by a myriad of bleak concrete buildings.

"Nadine," said Hillary. Nadine unresponsively stared out the window. "Nadine," said Hillary again, her body twisting so she could face her friend in the back.

"Uh, yeah?" said Nadine half-heartedly. The sky outside was gray in the predawn light.

"Ted sucked," said Hillary emphatically. Her mouth was smudged with last night's lipstick. "I didn't want to say any-thing because I knew he was your first boy, but he totally sucked. I know I'm not one to judge. I've dated my share of Teds, but chin up. Now you don't have to go to all those stupid soccer games."

"Mmmm," said Nadine as she released a large sigh. "He was beautiful, though."

"Someday, you'll meet someone who's beautiful and doesn't suck," said Hillary, her eyes wide with conviction.

"Like me!" said Jerome cheerily from the driver's seat.

"Thanks for the ride," said Nadine dismissively. They were pulling up to her house now. Nadine got out of the car and slowly headed to the front door, dragging her feet with each step. She paused to acknowledge the sunrise. The sky was shifting from gray to a pretty orange.

"Hey!" said Hillary running up beside Nadine.

"Did I leave something in the car?" said Nadine confused as she looked at Hillary's empty hands.

"No, I'm coming with you," said Hillary putting her arm around Nadine's icy shoulders. "We can talk about it, we can not talk about it, but I am yours for the day. You will need to lend me some clothes, though." Hillary made a sweeping gesture with her other hand at the tight emerald green dress she wore. The white sedan pulled away, and the two girls were left together in front of the house.

"Oh, thanks," said Nadine. She took the spare key from the mailbox and unlocked the stiff front door. "Hillary, that boat was a disaster. I thought it would be so perfect, we would have this amazing night together, and then I would lose my virginity, but it all went to hell. I want to tell you more about it, but I need a tampon and Midol stat. Thank God for my period. Otherwise, I would have had sex with that beautiful dick-brained *devil*."

"Oh honey, you got your period on the boat?" said Hillary, tenderly stroking the back of Nadine's head.

Goosebumps covered Nadine's bare skin as they entered the house. "I'm going to wait," said Nadine, walking into the entryway. "I know it's not cool, but I'm going to wait to have sex."

Since Nadine's parents volunteered at a soup kitchen Saturday mornings, it was empty inside the house except for the Virgin Mary in her portrait. The painting was serene, but in the light of the sunrise coming through the window, Mary's eye seemed to twinkle.

"Do what makes you happy!" said Hillary, following Nadine down the hallway to the bathroom, past a picture of Noah's ark with the animals lining up in pairs.

"Also, I'm never going anywhere without a tampon! From now on, I carry a tampon with me everywhere I go. And I'm waiting for the right person before I have sex. I deserve to be loved, and I am *no one's* arm candy. Now excuse me, but I'm bleeding like a dog in heat and hell to anyone who tells me to hold that, or anything else, in!"

With that, Nadine shut the bathroom door, got a tampon from under the sink, and inserted it into her vagina.

CHAPTER FIVE

STUCK

"Excuse me?" Keona weakly said as she approached what appeared to be a gangly teenage boy at the laminate front desk. As she got closer, Keona swallowed hard and realized despite the pimples, he was older than she'd originally thought.

"Yes, ma'am, how can I help you," the lanky front desk worker responded.

"Do you have any feminine products?"

He looked at her, confused.

"Do you need extra soap or body wash? I can have room service bring you some," he said.

"No," Keona responded, shuffling in place. She felt a chill as an older couple entered the lobby and was suddenly acutely aware of having gone downstairs bra-less. The thick material of her plaid pajama set felt thinner than silk. Keona leaned in to speak in an almost whisper as the older couple had come up to wait behind her. "Pads? Period products?"

"Oh," said the desk attendant as his brow furrowed. "Let me check." He disappeared, and Keona was left to wait. She stood, her arms wrapped tightly around her body in an attempt at camouflage as the gray-haired couple behind her

tittered away. A few agonizing minutes later, the desk attendant came back with a single utilitarian cardboard tube.

"Do you have any pads?" Keona asked, her voice hushed.
"I've never really used a tampon..."

"No, this is all I've got," said the man factually.

Keona grimaced as she took the tube.

"The twenty-four-hour CVS may have something. It's a
five-minute drive," he said at full volume. The couple behind
had stopped chatting, and the generically beige lobby tile
echoed his voice.

"Oh, is that walkable?"

"It's about twenty minutes, but I wouldn't recommend it
at night."

"Ah, I guess I'll have to try this then." Keona stared,
unmoving, at the tube in her hand.

"Have a great stay," said the man mechanically.

"Yeah, thanks," Keona responded limply and then wandered back through the mazelike hallways to the safety of
her hotel room.

Keona was staying with her best friend Nalani in a Holiday Inn in Colorado. When Keona got back to their shared
room, Nalani was sitting on the crisp white sheets painting
her toenails blue.

"I'm back, and I have a single tampon. What should I do?"
asked Keona, holding up the mass-produced cardboard tube.

Nalani barely glanced up from her toes. Their color was
lackluster in the dim hotel room lamplight.

Keona had always been a bit weirded out by tampons.
Nalani's mom Malia had given Nalani her first tampon
shortly after her first period, but no one had been there to
give Keona a tampon. By the time Nalani offered her one,
they were fourteen, and Keona had decided she was better off

sticking to pads. Keona didn't want her dad finding a bloody tampon in the trash, and she didn't want to risk dying from toxic shock syndrome, even if that risk was extremely low.

"They didn't have pads, or you didn't ask?" said Nalani as she swished at her toes with the nail polish.

The room simmered with the burning odor, making Keona a bit lightheaded. "I asked. I even told the front desk guy I'd never used tampons before. Nothing but embarrassment." Keona had taken her slippers off and now paced barefoot between the two beds, frequently turning with the grace of a kindergartener.

"Yikes. So now we can ask Ori to drive us to CVS? I'd love some Mike and Ikes," said Nalani.

Ori, Keona's father, was staying down the hall. His room had a slightly different view of the hotel's parking lot.

"No," said Keona. "You know he won't let you get Mike and Ikes. And he's got that meeting tomorrow. I don't want to bug him." She continued pacing.

"What you mean is you refuse to talk with your single father about your period." Nalani jammed the polish brush into the bottle, twisting it closed. The fact the polish hadn't splattered over the bedspread was a small miracle. "Well then, the choice is clear. You'll need to lose your tampon virginity or free bleed in your hotel bed. What will it be?"

"I'm not free bleeding!" moaned Keona. In all honesty, Keona would have preferred free-bleeding to the tampon, but what if the hotel charged her father for the ruined sheets? He'd probably make her pay for them with interest to teach her about responsibility.

"Really? Yay! Buh-bye, Keona's tampon virginity. Next will be your actual virginity. I hope you don't wait another sixteen years!" Nalani wriggled her wet toes and gave Keona's hip a friendly punch as she walked by.

"Yeah yeah, says the fellow virgin," said Keona as she headed to the bathroom, attempting to shrug off her friend's comments.

Keona spent a few minutes on the toilet examining the cardboard tube and the overtly pink paper packaging before gently attempting to shove the tampon into her vagina. When that failed, she applied additional force. Still no success. All she felt was irritated swelling flesh.

Keona hoisted herself onto the bathroom counter and seated herself in a sort of crab position. Once there, she began investigating her vagina as best she could in the poor lighting. One hand split open the two sets of lips to reveal two side-by-side holes ringed with blood, one larger than the other. *Huh, I didn't know the pee hole was so close to the vagina,* Keona thought.

Keona called out to her friend, "I can't get it in. It feels like I'm hitting a brick wall."

"What angle are you trying?" called Nalani back.

"Angle? Straight up, so 0°."

"Should be 45°," called Nalani.

"Thanks," called Keona. *Really, they couldn't mention that in health class?*

Still atop the counter, Keona attempted to maneuver the tampon's applicator into the larger of the two holes while monitoring it visually in the mirror. It was a tight fit, but this time the cardboard began to insert a few centimeters. Keona pushed the lever of the applicator and felt the tampon abrasively ram into her vagina.

All or nothing, thought Keona and kept pushing painfully until the entire tampon was sequestered in her flesh.

Soon, only the white string hung from the larger hole. Keona washed her hands thoroughly and left the bathroom, waddling a bit.

"Congratulations on your first tampon!" said Nalani. "You can now go swimming on your period. So, TV?"

"Yes to TV, but you should know they make period swimsuits," muttered Keona. *Kinda like swimming diapers for babies, but still better than this.* She squirmed a little, feeling the tampon inside of her.

Nalani turned on the TV and began flipping through channels. Its bright light flickered in the room.

"One more thing, make sure to replace that with a fresh one when you wake up. Mostly I don't want you getting toxic shock and dying. But also in full transparency, I don't want to miss a ski day," said Nalani.

Keona snorted. "Neither do I."

***

When the sun rose the next morning, Keona tiptoed to the bathroom, nervous she'd already had the tampon in too long. Keona automatically peed first thing in the morning, but today that meant she peed on the tampon's string.

Shit, of course, I did that. Keona stared at the pee-saturated string hanging above the shallow toilet bowl. She grabbed some toilet paper and gently grasped the string, and tugged. Keona felt the tampon begin to budge, when the feeling was replaced with pain. Keona stopped pulling, then gently tugged a second time. Again, a terrible aching pain. It was as if someone was pinching her vagina with malice.

Keona scrambled onto the bathroom counter yet again and situated herself in the crab pose. Spreading open both sets of wrinkled pink lips, she looked to where the tampon string entered her vagina.

What's that? Thought Keona as she noticed the flesh caught on the now red tampon. It was difficult to make out in the dank bathroom light, but it appeared as if the fleshy bit between the two holes she'd seen yesterday was caught and twisted with the tampon string. *Oh no,* thought Keona, *did I put it in wrong? Is this the wrong hole? Oh God, how did this even happen?*

Keona washed her hands, heavy on the soap to remove the smell, and then went to her friend asleep in a bed. Nalani's snores harmonized with the ancient heating unit under the window. Keona grabbed Nalani's shoulder and shook it slightly. Nalani was an infamously heavy sleeper.

"Five more minutes," croaked Nalani from the bed with her eyes still peacefully closed.

"Lani, I need your help. Please wake up," said Keona shaking her friend's shoulder. "Seriously, the tampon's stuck, and I need you. The bit between the two holes is twisted on the string."

Nalani's head turned on the pillow, and her eyes cracked open. She looked blearily at her friend through a mane of wild bedhead.

"I have no idea what you're saying, but yank it out, and you'll be fine." Nalani's eyes began to flutter closed once again as her head burrowed into the overstuffed hotel pillow.

"*Lani,* it's stuck! I can't yank it out." Keona's trembling voice quickly grew louder.

"Stop yelling. I'm awake," moaned Nalani. "Just pull harder. If the tampon hasn't soaked in a lot of blood, there will be some rug burn."

"You're not listening. The tampon is drenched in blood. It's caught on the skin!" Keona's hands gesticulated frenetically.

"What do you mean it's caught on the skin?"

"Between the two holes."

Nalani looked up at Keona quizzically. Keona's face was sweaty and unblinking. Behind Keona, the sunrise was a caustic orange.

"It's caught between your vagina and butthole?" said Nalani, propping herself up on an elbow. "Why would you pull toward your butthole? Pull forward, not back, Keke. Literally the same 45° angle it went in."

Keona leaned in inches from Nalani's face, glowering. "Not my butthole! My vagina and the smaller hole right next to it. The pee hole, you know! The urethra."

"First, backup, you've got morning breath. Second, what are you talking about? The pee hole is tiny. How could it be caught on the pee hole? "

"The small bit between the two holes is caught on the string."

"Rewind. Explain to me in detail how you inserted the tampon yesterday."

Keona began pacing anxiously between the two beds, going to and from the nightstand.

"I took a look and found the hole, the bigger one of the two, and then I put the tampon into the larger hole at a 45° angle. Now the bit between is caught in the tampon string, and hasn't this ever happened to you?"

"You have two holes, and your tampon is caught on a bit between them?" said Nalani tentatively.

Keona was exasperated, her face red, and she was breathing heavily. "*Yes*, between the two holes! Do I have to keep repeating myself?"

Nalani stared at her friend. "There's only *one* hole."

Keona stopped pacing, and they looked into each other's eyes. Keona looked as if she was somehow both choking and frozen in time.

"I mean, there's the butthole in the back," continued Nalani, "and there is a pee hole somewhere, but that hole's so tiny I can't even see where the pee leaves my body. There's no way that hole should be involved in tampons. If it is, I think you really need to see a doctor."

Keona sat on the edge of her bed and began rocking back and forth. "Oh God, oh God, there's something wrong with me."

Nalani moved beside her, wrapping Keona's shoulder with her arm in a sort of hug. "You're going to be fine. I'm sure a doctor will be able to help. You just need to get the tampon out, and then you can shove some toilet paper in your underwear until we get to a store." Keona continued to rock.

"I'm not sure how to get it out… Can you help me?" Keona didn't want her friend inspecting her vagina, but what else could she do? She desperately needed help getting the tampon out, and the only way Keona could see that happening was for Nalani to have a close-up of her untamed bush.

"Keke, you can do this without me! You don't want my help. You got it in there. *You* can get it out."

"But I can't get it out! Please help me," begged Keona, her voice overflowing with emotion.

"I honestly can't. I think I'd vomit. I'm still having flashbacks to that fetal pig from bio. You know I fainted and had nightmares for weeks." Nalani's face went pale at the memory.

"Dissecting a fetal pig and helping me get this stuck tampon our are very different. Please!" compelled Keona. She stared wide-eyed into Nalani's soul.

"It's a pink fleshy thing with blood. Can't do it. Hell no. I'm sorry, but if you need help, we should get Ori. He can take you to the ER."

With the mention of her father, Keona recoiled. "Fuck!" swore Keona. "We *are not* telling my father."

"Then you'll need to get the tampon out." Nalani began braiding her hair as Keona closed her eyes tightly to think. "Honestly, Keona, your dad can handle it. Going to the ER, it's not that big a deal. We'll miss skiing, but that'll be the worst of it."

"Do not tell my father," said Keona, her voice steely with resolve. "I'd rather die." Then she paused to think.

Keona's father had been a single parent on and off for the last ten years since Keona's mom had passed away. He'd remarried when Keona was nine, but then Keona's stepmom had filed for divorce almost three years ago. She quickly disappeared from both their lives, and Keona never knew why. Ori had always been a firm believer in self-reliance, and losing his second wife to divorce had reinforced this mantra. If "till death do us part" didn't mean anything, then you couldn't count on anyone but yourself.

"I have a compromise so we can fix this, not tell my father, and go skiing today," stated Keona. "I need you to hold my phone, so the flashlight is on my vagina. If you're worried about vomiting, you can keep your eyes closed and hold your breath. The lighting in the bathroom is useless, and I can't fully see what's going on in order to get the tampon out. Will you do that for me, shine the light? You're my best friend, and we both want to go skiing today." Keona sat on the edge of the bed, her toes digging into the thin carpeting underneath. Sunlight burned in the room, useless without a mirror.

Nalani scowled then said, "Fine, but if this doesn't work, you promise to immediately ask Ori to take you to a doctor? I'm worried for you."

Keona shuddered at the mention of her father but slowly nodded.

They marched into the bathroom. Nalani squeezed her eyes closed, holding her phone's flashlight up. Keona removed her underwear before returning to the crab position for the third time.

Keona examined her vagina methodically like it was indeed a fetal pig, and she didn't know where to make the first incision. She prodded the fleshy mess of hair, skin, and string. It didn't help.

"Oh God, I'm gonna regret this, but if you want me to take a look and see if I've misinterpreted this whole 'two-hole situation' into something more than it is, I'll do it," said Nalani, her eyes still closed as tightly as the doors of a bomb shelter.

"Yes, please," said Keona. The bathroom counter was cold plastic, and her skin stuck to it as she moved her body.

"Looking now, but if I faint, you owe me like a dozen manicures," said Nalani.

"Duh," said Keona. Keona watched as Nalani's eyes gradually opened, squinting at the train wreck between Keona's legs.

"Oh fuck, what is that?" gawked Nalani.

"Fuck," said Keona. "Stop staring!"

Nalani instantly shut her eyes. "Your vagina is definitely not normal, Keona. We're best friends, and we have been for ten years, so I'm telling it to you straight. That shit's mutated."

"Got it. Now quiet, please, and stop moving the light. I need to get this out." Keona had given up on pulling the tampon out because every time she tried, the little flap of skin between the holes resistant with excruciating pain. Instead, she now tried pushing it farther into her vagina. *I should have cut my nails before this trip*, she thought. With the tampon farther in, she was able to extricate the string from the strap of skin between the two holes across her vagina.

It felt like an eternity as Keona tried to remove the tampon. But she couldn't. It was stuck, like a stiletto in the mud if that mud was quicksand.

"I'm really sorry, but my arm's getting sore," said Nalani after ten minutes. "Any closer to getting it out?"

"No."

"Okay, time to tell Ori," said Nalani, lowering her arm. The two stayed there in somber silence.

"Fine, but I need to go to the bathroom first," said Keona.

Nalani left, the door closing soundly behind her. Keona was now alone in the dim bathroom light. She wiped herself, and the toilet paper was dry and thin, scratching at her irritated flesh.

"This is a shithole of a hotel. It has single-ply toilet paper. No pads. No lighting. Toilet paper made of knives. It's their fucking fault," Keona muttered to herself. The blood rushed in her head like a pounding concert she didn't want to be at. She splashed some cold water on her face. *What will my dad do?*

***

Time felt fragile, slowing down and speeding up at random, until there they were knocking at Ori's hollow door.

"Running early for breakfast, aren't we girls? Good!" said Ori, letting them in. Ori, a heavyset man, wore his ski clothes and slippers, mostly ready for the day an hour early. The clothes rustled as he moved about, grabbing his wallet with its frayed stitching off the desk

Keona's face was hot and sticky, like a fake leather car seat parked in the sun too long. Nalani stood by her side, her hand rubbing Keona's shoulder through the coarse fabric of her shirt. They had changed before coming to Ori's room into long-sleeve shirts and joggers. Good "ER clothes."

"Sir, I have an emergency, and I need you to take me to an urgent care or a hospital," said Keona quickly before she lost her nerve.

Ori looked at his daughter, analyzing her from top to bottom as if his eyes were an X-ray machine. His face had a quizzical expression. He said nothing.

The teens waited.

"You don't appear to be bleeding," said Ori sharply.

Keona heard Nalani cough, probably a cover for Nalani's awkward laugh reflex. They stood in place.

"No," said Keona. Ori's room was cold, the AC at full blast, and Keona tried not to shiver.

"Are you high?" asked Ori sternly, his lips two shriveled worms on his face, smashed together.

"No," said Keona.

"Well?" said Ori glaring.

"I need a medical professional to remove a tampon trapped in my vagina," said Keona. She glanced at the window, longing to be anywhere but here. Outside, people dressed to ski were exiting the hotel in droves. Ori took a minute to consider this new information.

"Is that something that can happen?" asked Ori, now lasering in on Nalani with his eyes. "Something that requires medical attention and in no way can be dealt with at home?"

"In this case, yes, sir," said Nalani. "She's already done everything she can independently do to get it out."

Ori thought for another minute.

Keona held her breath and tried to focus on the window. More and more people seemed to be streaming out of the hotel. They all seemed to be in black or red. It was like a sea of ants leaving a collapsing anthill, and she was still trapped inside.

"Okay, grab your jackets, and we'll go," said Ori.

***

The drive to the urgent care had been depressing. All around them was perfect, untouched powdery snow while Keona and Nalani sat in the backseat of a discount-rental car with food wrappers poking out of the seatback pocket. Ori sat upfront, like a disgruntled police officer transporting a couple of miscreants to the station.

After parking and entering, Keona and Ori stood in the blindly white Urgent Care room as Nalani bided time in the waiting area.

After a painful eight minutes in silence, a woman in her mid-thirties entered the room where Keona and Ori waited. The woman had curly hair that framed her asymmetrical eyes, one almost half an inch lower than the other.

"Hello, my name is Carla. How can I help you today?" Carla was wearing baggy seafoam green scrubs and looked a bit like an anthropomorphized glob of toothpaste.

After a slight pause, Ori spoke. "My daughter is having an issue. She will explain." Ori stood tall as if a rod were thrust through his spine while Keona shifted back and forth from foot to foot. The room was almost claustrophobic, with the three of them standing in the small space between the doctor's exam table and the almost empty white desk and chair.

"Umm, can I have some privacy with the doctor?" asked Keona softly.

"I'm actually a physician's assistance," interjected Carla cheerily.

"Fine," said Ori to Keona, "but I will be talking to this… 'physician's assistant'… after." Ori stalked out of the room, decisively closing the door behind him.

Keona let go of a breath she didn't know she'd been holding. "Can I sit?" she asked Carla, who nodded and gestured to the examination table.

"Of course," said Carla. "So what's going on, Keona?"

The room seemed to expand, and Keona noticed a painting of rainbow balloons on one wall.

"Okay, so before I tell you this, you should know that I 110 percent don't want to be here, but the situation is dire." Keona sat on the paper-covered bedding, and it crinkled as she wobbled from side to side. *I need to tell her everything. This is my only chance.*

"So I, umm, have two holes in my vagina. Or a broken pee hole. Or like a mutation. Unclear what's wrong, but something's *very wrong.*" Keona spoke fast, as if her words were accelerating out of her mouth. "When I used pads, it was never a problem, but now my tampon, my first tampon, by the way, because the stupid concierge at the stupid hotel didn't have pads, is stuck even though I tried *so hard* to get it out. It's stuck, and when I try and get it out, it hurts. Like *really* fucking hurts. Nalani, my friend, looked, and now we both know something's definitely wrong. This is a waking nightmare because I had to tell my father, and he's going to kill me. Or make me go work on a farm to pay off the debt from this visit because I don't know how much this is going to cost, but my father believes in fixing your own mistakes. Sorry, that was off topic. I'm just screwed because of a stupid tampon. Sorry for swearing. Yeah, sorry. Shit. Sorry."

"Take a deep breath," said Carla while condescendingly miming taking a deep breath.

Keona continued panting like an overheating purebred pug.

"Let me see if I got this straight. You're having an issue involving your vagina?"

"Yes," confirmed Keona between hurried breaths.

"And you believe there's a tampon trapped inside your vagina."

"Yes! I don't believe, *it's there.* I put it there last night, and now it's stuck in my pussy! Not that I ever use the term pussy, sorry. Is pussy a bad word? Oh, God."

"Time for another deep breath." Carla mimed again, this time more slowly. "You and I are getting on the same page, but I need you to slow down. Now, there appears to be a tampon trapped inside of your vagina by what you believe is a deformity."

"Correct, it's mutated."

"Let's not jump to any conclusions, Keona. Everyone's vulva and vagina are unique and change during puberty. Why don't you take off your pants, and I'll take a look?"

Keona removed her pants and then her navy Walmart briefs before sitting back on the table.

"Ah, I see the problem here," said Carla, her face now between Keona's hair-dotted legs.

Keona could smell Carla's eucalyptus mint shampoo, and it cooled her nostrils as she tried the obnoxious deep breaths Carla had previously recommended.

"So," said Carla popping her head up to look Keona in the eyes, "you have a septate hymen. A septate hymen is a congenital birth defect that will make things like tampons and sex difficult. I'm guessing you're not sexually active?"

"No," said Keona, her toes wiggling. *Why does it matter if I'm sexually active?*

"You may want to get this fixed before you have any form of penetrative sex. Otherwise, there may be a large amount of blood and pain. In nonmedical terms, your hymen didn't properly open up before you were born and is separating the vaginal opening into two smaller holes. The tampon you inserted into one of those two smaller holes has now physically expanded with blood and is now larger than the opening, making it difficult to remove. Let me get some tools to get this out, and I'll be right back, okay?"

Keona nodded, and Carla pulled a curtain around her before leaving the office.

***

A week later, Keona was home and studying in her bedroom when a knock at the door interrupted her concentration.

"It's unlocked."

Ori opened the door.

"Let's talk in the living room?" said Ori gruffly, and Keona followed him out.

The living room contained three pieces of furniture: a sturdy green couch, a brown recliner, and a coffee table Keona's grandfather had built. The only decoration was a single framed picture of Keona with her grandparents, who had since passed away. Dust had collected on the wood floor since Keona's latest monthly vacuuming (vacuuming being of her many chores). Ori insisted she do chores so she would be independent and know how to take care of herself.

They sat, Keona on the couch and Ori on his unreclined recliner. The room smelled and sounded like a library, musky and quiet, which made sense given the number of books and old newspapers piled on the coffee table. There was no TV, only an old radio among the books.

"We need to talk about what happened last week," said Ori.

Do we? Last week, after Carla had delicately and painfully removed the blood-soaked tampon from Keona's vagina, Keona had sat in the waiting room wearing a diaperlike pad from the Urgent Care while Ori and Carla talked for what seemed like forever. Then, Ori had taken Keona and Nalani to a Walmart where he'd bought her pads, and they all shared a soggy pizza. Keona had truly hoped that would be the end of it.

"Carla, the not-a-doctor from the Urgent Care, explained to me you were born with a minor birth defect that can be corrected with outpatient surgery. I need you to know if you would like that surgery. I can change our insurance plan for next year, so it's mostly covered, and then I can pay for any additional cost."

"Oh," said Keona. The couch was hard underneath her and grounded her to reality while her head spun in circles.

"While I'm a firm believer in paying for one's own mistakes, you have made no mistakes," said Ori firmly. "I do not expect you, a minor, to pay to have a birth defect corrected." Ori paused as if there was more to say, but nothing came out for a while. "I have to elect the healthcare plan soon, so I expect you to have an answer by next week."

"Yes, sir," said Keona automatically, her brain still in a fog of information.

"I have also spoken with Malia, and she has agreed to talk with you through your decision," said Ori referencing Nalani's mother. "You wouldn't expect a toad to teach you how to swim. You'd ask a frog. Malia will be your swim teacher. Understood?"

"Understood."

"Good," said Ori, "you're dismissed." The recliner squealed as he leaned back. Ori turned on the old radio in front of him, and from it came voices chatting merrily about a new baseball player.

Keona ran to her room. Grabbing her phone, she texted Nalani, "Oh my gosh, they can fix me!" Then she fell into her bed, exhausted but grinning fervently. *Everything's going to be okay. I can't believe he's going to make everything okay.*

Through the thin walls of the house, Keona could hear sizable cheering on the radio. *Must be a home run. That'll make him happy. Ya know, he deserves to be happy. He really is doing his best for us. Sometimes life gives us lemons, or a divorce, or a tampon. All we can do with it is our best. Or, as dad would say, find a frog and learn to swim.*

CHAPTER SIX

CHEERS TO THAT

———

Frances woke up in the morning splayed across her college-issued twin mattress, still wearing her sweaty clothes from the night before, a pulling-at-the-seams black top, and parachute pants. The stained comforter and blotchy top sheet lay crumpled on the ground next to the bed, partially concealing a pile of dozens of crumpled aluminum cans. The room smelled musty.

Frances hadn't gotten a lot of sleep, and now her alarm was blaring from its perch atop unused textbooks. 7 a.m.

The night before, Frances had gone out with her friends on a Tuesday, which was always a highly regrettable thing to do. *Nobody sane goes out on Tuesdays*, thought Frances. Frances swore to herself she hadn't had that much to drink, only a glass of deep red wine or maybe two. *And a round of shots at the club. Only one round, maybe.* It was her stupid friends' fault. They had ordered multiple bottles of wine for the table on a Tuesday. *My friends are assholes.*

Frances wasn't sure if someone had refilled her glass when she wasn't looking or if she had poured herself extra wine to spite their stupidity. After all, she had been splitting the bill. Then, after all the wine, these same stupid friends dragged her to an empty club *on a Tuesday* where they blasted the AC despite the low occupancy. It had been arctic inside. At the club, a pasty Eastern European bro, resembling a Bond villain in all black, had tried to talk to Frances about his pretentious start-up. He had stood too close to her for what felt like an hour and then coughed in her face. After pulling herself away from the tech bro, Frances had made her way back to her dorm sometime between one and two in the morning.

Once home, she remembered going to the bathroom, plopping down on her bed for a minute, and thinking, *standing up is not an option*. Hell, if she had stood up, she would have definitely puked. Clearly, that was a result of the stupid Thai food that never agreed with her. When Frances had closed her eyes, the room hadn't been spinning or anything, only a little wobbly like the Caribbean cruise she'd gone on for Spring Break. Frances had hated that cruise. The endless cocktails had all been way too fruity with not enough rum. No, the nausea last night was definitely because of the stupid Thai food. *Asshole friends keeping me up all night and getting me sick*, Frances concluded.

Now it was, unfortunately, daylight. Frances got up, grabbed a fresh tampon, and headed to the bathroom down the narrow hallway. She took a seat in a cubicle, staring blearily at the graffitied door in front of her without much comprehension. After peeing, she sat for a minute. No way she was going to shower today. *Way too much effort*, she thought. Frances pulled her current tampon out. While putting the tampon in the small feminine products receptacle, she noticed the tampon was white as a blank page with barely a speck of blood.

This was bizarre. Frances didn't have a crazy heavy flow, but her tampons were always particularly bloody on the second day of her period. Frances racked her brain, trying to remember the night before. She vaguely recalled putting a tampon in, but she didn't remember taking the previous tampon out. *No. I didn't. It's not possible*, thought Frances.

Or was it? Could she really fit two tampons up there? No way. Maybe?

Hesitantly, Frances inserted her pinky finger into her vagina. It was a bit dry from the tampon, so the finger went in with uncomfortable friction. This wasn't a typical Wednesday morning, but Frances had to know if something was up there. The first inch, she didn't feel anything.

As Frances's pinky's middle knuckle slowly passed her inner labia, she felt it. Something hard. Something deep in there. A second tampon?

"Oh shit!" Frances gasped. Quickly pulling her finger out, she reached for her phone before realizing her hand had vagina juice on it.

Rushing out of the stall, Frances washed her hands and found her gynecologist's phone number.

"Hi, do you take emergency appointments?" said Frances on the phone, sounding a lot calmer than she felt. She thought she could still smell the vagina juice on her phone as she held it to her face.

"Yes, but depending on the emergency, you may need to call 911," said the nurse on the other line. "Do you mind if I ask what the emergency is?"

"I put two tampons in, and the first one is stuck all the way up there. I don't feel a string!" Frances felt the hairs on the back of her neck as she said the problem aloud for the first time. She hurriedly looked at the four-stall doors to check they were all open and the stalls unoccupied.

"Ah, I see. Have you experienced any of the symptoms of toxic shock? Flulike symptoms, diarrhea, or dizziness?" the nurse asked, sounding like a dispassionate waiter listing the evening specials.

"No, nothing. Some nausea, but I had Thai food yesterday... and some alcohol," said Frances. Looking in the bathroom mirror, Frances saw her own smudged eyeliner and smeared lipstick.

"Hmm, If you can get here in the next thirty minutes, we can fit you in for a quickie with Doctor Blitz."

Frances wasn't sure if she imagined hearing judgment in the woman's tone, but she didn't care. She didn't even laugh at the idea of a gynecologist giving her a quickie. She wanted the tampon out, and she wanted it out *now*.

"I'll be there," said Frances, and after hanging up, she shoved her phone in the deep pockets of the flowy pants.

Frances sprinted out of the dorm. As she speed-walked to the doctor's office, her phone jingled, and without thinking, she picked it up.

"Hey girl," said Janine casually, "didn't see you at spin this morning. Lunch in the dining hall?" Janine and Frances usually grabbed lunch at noon when they both had a break from class.

"I'm heading to an appointment, but I should be there for lunch," said Frances trying not to sound too out-of-breath as she walk-ran to her gyno. "How on earth did you spin this morning?" she continued dubiously. It was colder outside than Frances had thought, and her stomach ached dully as her feet pounded the pavement in a thin pair of ballet flats.

"Duh, I left last night after dinner when y'all decided to go to the club," said Janine. "You tried to drag me with, but there was no way I was going clubbing when we had spin today. Plus, Tuesday clubbing sucks."

"I forgot," said Frances.

"Obviously, you missed spin again," said Janine emphasizing her words, the judgment thick in her voice like a layer of fudge on an ice-cream Sunday.

Frances rolled her eyes. "I gotta run, Janine. I'll call you back."

"Sure," said Janine sounding unconvinced, and hung up.

Frances shoved the cracked phone back into her pocket and continued on to the doctor's office. Once there and in a room, a nurse handed her a blue medical gown and told her to change, making sure to take off everything except for her bra. That's when Frances realized she was still in last night's clothes and not wearing a bra. Her tight handkerchief top didn't leave room for such modesties.

Putting on the gown, Frances was completely naked under the light blue plastic cloth. Dried out mascara scratched at her palms as she rubbed her eyes. While most of the room was white, the floor was a pale blue checkerboard, and Frances felt that she and her matching blue gown might sink into it like quicksand and never be heard from again.

I bet Janine would be glad to be rid of me. Maybe I'd be better off in a new world starting fresh. No judgmental Janine or "friends" who get me blackout drunk on a Tuesday. I'd be better off without everyone else's bullshit, thought Frances.

"Hello, good to see you again, Frances," said Doctor Blitz entering the room. "What appears to be the problem today?" Frances always thought Doctor Blitz was much too pretty to be a gynecologist. She was probably in her late thirties, but her blonde hair and blue eyes brought to mind a life-size Barbie doll. A Barbie doll with a medical degree and the pristine white teeth of an LA native.

"I got a tampon stuck in my hoo-ha," said Frances, standing in the middle of the room and gesturing at her stomach.

"Oh no, why don't you get up on the table, and we'll take a look," said Doctor Blitz. "How did it get stuck?"

Frances confided in Dr. Blitz that she'd had a busy night and stuck two tampons up her vagina.

"Are you sure it's only one extra tampon stuck in there? Nothing else?" said Doctor Blitz in her sing-songy voice, "Better you tell me now than later."

"No. No. I don't think so…" Frances paused and tried to remember the night before. "Probably not? Could I even fit three tampons in there?"

"You'd be surprised," said Dr. Blitz as she chuckled to herself. Frances wasn't sure if she was reassured or more concerned. "I'll check for a third tampon, just in case." Dr. Blitz pulled latex gloves taut over her small hands.

Next, Frances's feet were in the stirrups, and the doctor was warning her she'd feel a slight pinch from the speculum.

The lubricant was cold, and the slight pinch was more like a carjack going up inside of her vagina, but Frances held firm. She never understood why Dr. Blitz said it would only be a 'small pinch.' It was never a 'small pinch.' Though Frances was no stranger to large packages being inserted into her vagina, the speculum was always a bitch.

"You know this happens all the time," Dr. Blitz said *casually*, her head between France's outspread legs.

"Really?" despite the pain, Frances liked the idea of her not being a drunken idiot and instead a totally regular woman who did things like putting two tampons in at the same time.

"Nope," said Doctor Blitz, "but I thought it might make you feel better. Okay, I've removed a tampon, and I'm checking if there's anything else in here. Count to thirty Mississippi, and this will all be over."

And after a painful thirty seconds, it was over. Dr. Blitz took out the speculum, and Frances removed her feet from the stirrups.

"Okay, we're done with the hard part," said Doctor Blitz while removing her gloves and washing her hands thoroughly. "Before I let you go, we need to talk toxic shock syndrome."

Frances almost groaned but was able to keep it in. She didn't want more judgment from Doctor Blitz. *I've already gotten a tampon stuck up my vagina. Do I really also need a lecture?* she thought.

Doctor Blitz continued, "While nothing can get lost in your vagina, what goes in will come out. Leaving a tampon in there for over eight hours can lead to toxic shock syndrome. Toxic shock syndrome is bad, and you don't want it. So, if you're going to go have a crazy night out and there's the possibility that you'll forget you have a tampon inserted, I'd recommend switching to pads," said Doctor Blitz. "Got it?"

Frances imagined Doctor Blitz on a night out. She was definitely a tampon-and-merlot-at-a-speakeasy type of woman. Frances wished she was more like Doctor Blitz but less sanctimonious.

"Yeah," Frances exhaled. "I definitely don't want to do this again. "

"I bet you don't! I'll leave now. You can use the attached bathroom to clean yourself up and get dressed. See you at your next annual visit, and hopefully no sooner!"

"I promise," said Frances as Doctor Blitz left the room. The room seemed to brighten at this conclusion, and the aching in Frances's vagina gradually faded away.

With that, Frances was left alone to go wipe wet lubricant off her groin and get dressed. As she pulled her clothes back on, they felt greasy and gross. She almost preferred the blue gown to being reminded of the night before.

I am never doing this again. I can do better. No tampons and no alcohol until I learn to be more responsible, thought Frances, looking at herself in the mirror as she washed her hands clean. Taking a wet piece of toilet paper, she rubbed around her eyes and mouth, removing as much of the remaining eyeliner and lipstick as she could. It was over. Now she only had to deal with her unwashed hair and missed classes.

Frances decided to walk home to clear her head and called Janine back along the way.

"Hey, sorry about that," said Frances, "I was at the doctor." Leaves on the trees were the color of Florida oranges, and the air smelled like fresh rain.

"Didn't know you had a doctor's appointment today. You sure were leading the charge last night," said Janine flippantly.

Frances wanted to fight back, to say it was someone else's fault, but now she remembered she had indeed been the one who'd suggested clubbing and tried to make Janine come with. It was time to start being honest with herself. If she couldn't take Janine's judgment, then was she any better than the rest of her shitty friends? Frances's flats bent on the rocky cobblestone, twisting her feet as she walked.

"I didn't have an appointment," said Frances as she hopped over a puddle. "I put two tampons in last night and had to go to the gyno this morning to get the second one removed." Frances braced herself for Janine's laughter. There was no reason to expect sympathy from Janine, who had her shit together and wanted people to know it. When the laughter didn't come, Frances was confused.

"That's annoying. I've put a second one in a couple of times. It's a pain, but I've always been able to get it out myself."

"The gyno said it didn't happen much," said Frances, her voice inflecting up at the end of the sentence, signaling an unasked question. If Janine, with her shit together, could put in two tampons, why was it so bad that she, Frances, had made the same mistake late at night?

"Maybe people don't go to the gyno to remove them, but I know for a fact that ladies accidentally put multiple tampons in all the time," said Janine, her voice level, not realizing the significance of the statement. "The trick for getting them out is to bear down hard. It always works."

They continued talking, but Frances's mind drifted off. *Was the debacle this morning my fault for being too drunk last night, or is my drinking absolutely fine and the gyno trip a commonplace accident?* she wondered. Eventually, the conversation ended, and Frances was left with her thoughts and the noise of the wind to keep her company. *Doctor Blitz was kind of a bitch,* she thought. *Everyone at that office was so condescending.*

When finally home, Frances was excited to wash off last night, including the club sweat and guilt. After showering, Frances brushed her teeth and her hair, put on a pad and some pajamas, and got under the bed covers. She knew that these were the things she should have done twelve hours ago. Instead, it was almost 10 a.m. After setting an alarm, she took a twenty-minute snooze.

Waking up feeling refreshed under the covers, Frances unfurled her yoga mat and did fifty crunches in spite of the soreness in her stomach. Getting dressed in a cardigan and her interview-ready black skirt, Frances prepared for her 11 a.m. lecture. She'd missed spin and her 9 a.m., but that wasn't going to happen again.

Frances collected the crumpled cans from the floor into a bag, thoughtfully adding her box of tampons to the mix. On her way out the door, Frances grabbed the handle of vodka from under her bed. Once in the bathroom, she tossed the empty cans and tampons in the large bathroom garbage can and then poured what vodka remained in the handle in a toilet bowl. There wasn't much left, but flushing it still gave Frances satisfaction.

Yes, maybe Barbie Doctor Blitz made me feel worse about the tampon than she'd needed to, but I am responsible for how I treat myself and my body. From now on, I am on a cleanse, thought Frances.

Tossing the empty plastic vodka container into the garbage can, Frances smiled at her own makeup-free face in the spotless mirror. Leaving the bathroom, she held her head high and headed to class.

CHAPTER SEVEN

HORMONES

———

You're thirteen and covered in acne. Cry to your friends about it. Cry to your mom about it. Cry to your new dermatologist about it. The dermatologist mentions birth control can help with hormonal acne. Beg your mom for birth control. Mom says maybe. Mom talks to dad. Mom tells you dad said no. Beg dad for birth control. Dad says you're too young for birth control. Tell dad you hate him. Give dad the silent treatment for a month. Mom and dad agree you can get birth control when your fifteen if the acne is still a problem and you behave better. Begin speaking to dad again. Religiously apply every acne treatment, lotion, and concealer under the sun. Face remains red, splotchy, and rougher than a middle school bully. Cry frequently to the face in the mirror.

You're fifteen and still covered in acne. Go to your primary care doctor and beg for birth control to treat the war zone on your face. The doctor prescribes a combination pill. You take it religiously for the first couple of weeks but gradually become more relaxed. What's the difference between 8 p.m. and 9 p.m.? The acne fades from some of your face, and you cover what's left with large amounts of foundation. Boys begin to talk to you.

You're seventeen and dating your first boyfriend. You're both on the student newspaper, and you often make out in the newsroom when no one else is around. Your makeup rubs off on his face, so afterward, you go to the bathroom and apply another layer. He never comments on the makeup smeared all over his puffy cheeks, and you thank God for the similarity in your skin tones. On your six-month anniversary, you decide to give each other your virginities. He awkwardly puts on a condom, and you have sex in the park by your house after dark. You don't enjoy it, especially not the wet grass, but you tell him you do. You tell him you love him, and he says you'll be together forever. You have sex a couple more times, always with a condom.

You're eighteen when you leave for college. You and your boyfriend, whose puffy cheeks have now thinned into a chiseled jawline, decide to make a long-distance relationship work. Your boyfriend comes to visit you at your new college dorm. That night the condom breaks. You look at your birth control pack, and you've definitely missed a couple of pills. You google Plan B, a morning-after pill for pregnancy prevention, and discover you can still take it even though you're technically already on birth control. Your boyfriend goes to buy you Plan B, and while he's gone, you freshen up your makeup. You take Plan B. You vomit, and your head feels like it's being split in two by an ax. You tell your boyfriend he now has to use a condom and pull out every time. He says okay, but asks you to stop screaming. You didn't realize you were screaming. You fight over whether you were screaming. Your tears are murky and flesh-toned. Your boyfriend sleeps on the couch in the suite living room.

You're nineteen and suddenly single as fuck. Your ex-boyfriend has a new girlfriend less than a month after your breakup. Well, your most recent breakup. The final breakup. You stalk her on Instagram. Her skin is poreless. It must be a filter. You try to hookup with someone new. He asks to have sex, and you say no. This hookup leaves a blur of sweaty foundation smeared across his pale face. A month later, you try again. This new hookup also asks if you want to have sex. When you seem unsure, he says he's fine with anything. He wants you to be comfortable. You tell him you do want to have sex and ask him to use a condom. You're drunk, and the sex is pretty good. Actually, it's the best sex you've ever had. When you wake up, he smiles and asks for your number. His teeth are crooked. You give him a fake number. You never see him again.

You're twenty and dating your first real college boyfriend. Well, maybe boyfriend, maybe something else. What started as a hookup has bloomed into something, but you're not sure what. After four months of having sex a couple of times a week, you ask to define the relationship. This is the first man who's seen you in the harsh light of day without makeup on. It was an accident. You thought he'd left while you were in the shower, but for a brief instant, he saw you for you. He looks a little squinty-eyed as you ask about the relationship but agrees to be your "boyfriend." That night he asks to have sex without a condom. You tell him okay since you're on the pill, but he needs to pull out. He pulls out, and his viscous cum splatters across your bare chest. It's sticky. A few months later, you're on day thirty-one of your cycle, and you haven't gotten your period. You go to CVS and buy a pregnancy test. You pee on a stick. The stick says you're not pregnant. You get your period the next day. You break up with this "boyfriend." The next month you switch birth control pills. You like this generic better because you feel less cloudy, and your period comes on time every time.

You're twenty-one when you mention to your roommate you've been seeing pretty lights on and off for years now. She says it sounds like migraine auras and suggests you check if you're on the right birth control. On Google, you discover taking a combination oral contraceptive while having migraines with auras increases your likelihood of having a stroke. You don't want to have a stroke. You make a doctor's appointment. After telling the doctor about your headaches and answering some questions about your sexual activity and experience with the pill, the doctor recommends you get an IUD. Even though the doctor assures you all the IUDs are safe, you choose the copper IUD because it's hormone free, and you are still worried about having a stroke. Plus, you don't need the hormones now that your acne's mostly gone, fixed further by the myriad of products you bought from late-night infomercials. You faint after the IUD insertion, and your roommate has to come to pick you up from the office to walk you home. She's surprised you chose the copper IUD since it gave her horrible period pain. You cross your fingers and hope you don't cramp. Still, you think cramps would be better than a stroke.

You're twenty-seven, and you don't know a single other person on the copper IUD, but you think it's great. Everyone you meet who's tried the copper IUD has had problems with cramping, but for you, it just works. No more taking a pill every day. No more hormonal side effects. No more pregnancy tests. You still make your boyfriend wear a condom. You've been together for over a year now, and he tells you you're beautiful when you don't have any makeup on. You almost believe him.

CHAPTER EIGHT

LEAN ON ME

"Girl, you've had Botox, but you're judging my birth control?" said Shanice. Jasmine flushed slightly and stirred her acid-yellow margarita with its straw, so the ice clinked loudly. Then, she took a sip. A waitress delivered a specialty mimosa bucket, complete with champagne and colorful fruit juices, to the neighboring table. At their table, the three women had chosen to order separate drinks.

"Can I feel it?" asked Ashwini, reaching her hand out as Shanice offered her arm. The two were sitting next to each other across from Shanice at the Butter Muffin Cafe. "What's it called again?"

"Nexplanon," said Shanice. Ash tenderly felt Shanice's arm. Under the surface of Shanice's luxuriously soft skin, Ash felt a small Mike and Ike-shaped lump.

"My body is a temple," said Jasmine. "Just because I want to keep my face looking fresh doesn't mean I want to be a cyborg."

"Ignore her," said Ashwini, "she's just jealous we get laid."

"Oh yeah, still single and waiting on 'Mr. Right' aren't you?" goaded Shanice. Jasmine glared at her, though behind her large bug-eyed sunglasses, all that was visible was a slight scrunch of her nose. Jasmine's forehead didn't move. It never moved anymore.

"What have I missed?" asked Michelle striding up to the table, her large earrings jangling and her face bright with sunlight. With her vivid patterned sundress and quaffed hair, she looked totally in place among the cafe's vibrant cubist art and eclectic style.

"Michelle!" exclaimed Shanice and Ashwini in unison.

"Hi Mich," said Jasmine, pulling out the white wicker chair next to her. "It's sunny."

"I don't mind," smiled Michelle. "Boy, does this place smell good. Can't believe I haven't been here in a year." The smell of freshly fried beignets and sweet caramelized onions hung in the air. "Once we move into our new suite, we can come here together every single week!"

A year ago, before Michelle went abroad, Michelle, Jasmine, Shanice, and Ashwini had applied for housing together. After issues with their application last year (the application was nontransferable, and Michelle's last-minute study-abroad made her ineligible), a week ago, they'd been offered a prime remodeled suite with views of the town for the upcoming semester, but no one except Michelle had yet signed the paperwork. Housing for the school year was in the air.

"Can't believe you left us for an entire year!" proclaimed Shanice, her face lit up with an ear-to-ear smile. "I've missed you so much! You may have been in France, but there's nothing better than the Butter Muffin Cafe. I'll swear by it."

Michelle leaving for study abroad in France had strained the friend group of four. While their group friendship had formed in the marketing club freshman year, Shanice and Jasmine had actually been childhood friends who'd always had a touch-and-go relationship. The tension between the two had escalated in the last year after Shanice had a medical issue she used as an excuse to make demands on Jasmine. Then Ashwini, already sick of being in the middle of a war of words, had started dating her now boyfriend and had less time to act as a go-between.

For a while, it seemed like the three would go their separate ways. Only Michelle's monthly group calls from abroad had held them together. Her enthusiasm to hear details about each of her friends' loves, trials, and tribulations kept the friendship alive. It had taken a while, but Shanice and Jasmine had begun talking to one another again, though it was often far from pleasant. With Michelle back in town, this was their first in-person group meeting in a year. With only two weeks left to sign the paperwork for New Building, there was a lot of pressure for the brunch reunion to go well.

"I do miss the beignets," said Michelle, sniffing the air.

"Already ordered some for the table," said Ash while smiling, but the smile didn't quite reach her eyes.

"Shanice got a drug robot inserted into her arm," declared Jasmine.

"Says the girl with the pig-face implants," said Shanice, leaning forward across the table as if challenging Jasmine to a fistfight.

"It was *vegan!*" snapped Jasmine. The heads of the next table over turned toward them.

"Ladies, calm yourselves!" said Michelle, waving her hand between Jasmine and Shanice. "I want to hear all about this drug robot because I already know about Jas's Botox. I support all of y'all making your own decisions, though you should know I have the three most b-e-a-utiful friends and future roommates in all of the USA."

"What about your French friends?" asked Ashwini, giving Michelle side-eye. For a millisecond, Michelle's frowned before smiling again.

"Those hairy bitches?" said Shanice, leaning back into her seat. "No way they could compete. And it's not a robot. It's my new birth control. This little puppy lasts four years." Shanice pointed to where Ash had felt the Mike and Ike in her arm. "No way in hell am I getting pregnant before I WANT to be pregnant."

"Preach, girl," said Michelle.

A small puff of air angrily left Jasmine's nostrils.

It was a warm day, and all around them, other groups chatted away at their tables.

The waitress came up to the ladies to drop off their golden beignets, still steaming from the fryer. After taking Michelle's drink order and the table's order for food, the waitress bustled away, her ponytail bouncing like a bunny's bottom.

"I just can't believe, Shanice, you got this hormonal thing inserted permanently into your body after you had that terrible shot," said Jasmine, her voice punctuated with incredulity. "I may be harsh, but those chemicals drove you absolutely bonkers. You were crying in my bed for two weeks, and then you went all crashy and took pregnancy tests twice a day."

Shanice and Jasmine had stopped talking in the aftermath of Shanice's birth control shot. After a dozen pharmacy runs, Jasmine had gotten tired of chauffeuring a whiney and ungrateful Shanice to the drug store. When Shanice asked Jasmine to drive her to a Walgreens across town to buy a fourth box of pregnancy tests, Jasmine had cracked. She'd told Shanice, "I'll help you, but first, you need to stop whoring around like a two-buck prostitute or at least pay for gas with your hooker money."

What Jasmine had said in frustration as a joke did not make Shanice laugh. Instead, Shanice flew into a hormonal rage. The time Jasmine had spent helping Shanice, two weeks listening to her cry followed by a month of consoling her about a potential pregnancy, no longer mattered. To Shanice, Jasmine had transformed into a judgmental bitch who'd never been a true friend a day in their lives.

For months, Shanice complained about Jasmine to Ashwini at every opportunity, and this viewpoint was reinforced by Ashwini's confirmation that Jasmine was super judgy and not a great friend. During Michelle's monthly video calls, whenever Jasmine would extol the virtues of a new diet or vitamin, Ash would message Shanice "Neighhhh," a reference to Jasmine being on her high horse about everything.

Though Jasmine knew she had majorly overstepped when she had called out Shanice's sex life, Jasmine liked having a break from Shanice's crazy. Without Michelle as a buffer and with Shanice acting particularly needy, Jasmine had quickly become worn down. It was a relief suddenly not having to chauffeur around a crying and screaming friend. Jasmine enjoyed the newfound tranquility so much that she waited an entire month before apologizing to Shanice for the "whore" comment.

After Jasmine's delayed but genuine apology, the divide between the two only continued to grow. By then, neither really wanted to be friends anymore. What was the point? Jasmine rationalized that since Shanice had dropped out of the marketing club, the one activity they'd had together, and since Shanice was of late excessively needy and demanding, losing the friendship was no big loss. She conveniently overlooked their long history of slumber parties, shared secrets, and mutual trust.

For Shanice, the apology was too little too late. She remembered what her mom told her when she was young, "to have a friend is to be a friend," and Jasmine had failed this test miserably. No matter that Shanice herself hadn't been a supportive friend to Jasmine for months, this was clearly all Jasmine's fault. During this period, Ashwini was busy with her new boyfriend and only appeared every once in a while to take Shanice's side. Without Michelle to remind the group of the value of their friendship, Jasmine, Shanice, and Ashwini had drifted apart. Now they were physically back together again, allegedly to discuss the apartment opening at New Building.

"That was practically a year ago! I'm over it," said Shanice, her own glaring face reflecting back at her in Jasmine's sunglasses. "Yeah, the birth control shot was toxic, but I've had my period back for months now. I'm not going to stop having sex because you think I'm cheap, and I don't hear you offering to adopt my babies."

"She thinks we should all be nuns like her," said Ash, brushing some hair behind her shoulder.

"Just because I don't parade my pussy around town doesn't make me a nun," said Jasmine pursing her lips. "It makes me smart. Smarter than your bitchy ass."

"Ladies! I step back for a year, and y'all turned into feral cats," said Michelle. "Now, what's *really* going on here?"

"She's a drama queen," said Jasmine pointing at Ashwini, "always has been. And you, Shanice, I had to drop a class last year because I spent so much time listening to you cry and driving you around. In return, all you did was bitch at me. You're ungrateful and selfish. The two of you are horrible people." Ash guffawed, but Jasmine continued. "I'm sorry, Michelle, I'm glad you're back, but there's no way I could live with these backstabbers. I don't care how great New Building is. It's not worth it. If anything, I want out of this friend group! Not to live with them."

"Good riddance," said Ash.

"Stop it!" said Michelle.

"No, she's right," said Shanice. "Michelle, I don't think this is going to work. I'm sick of being told I should kiss Jas's feet because she's 'enlightened.' If she's such hot shit, she'd be a better friend instead of a judgmental bitch. Good friends don't kick you when you're down with a medical issue. I don't care if you apologized a month later. That's bullshit."

"What happened last year?" Michelle begged. The bitter smell of black coffee nearby engulfed the table.

"You want to know what happened?" said Jasmine, squarely facing Shanice across from her. "She cried, and cried, and cried in my room for weeks. I had to drive her to doctors' appointments and for vitamins and for pregnancy tests. I said *one* stupid thing after a month of being at her beck and call, and then she acts like I'm a villain. I was a goddamn saint!"

"You called her a whore and a prostitute!" said Ashwini, but no one looked at her except Jasmine, who turned diagonally across the table to face Ashwini.

"Oh and you," said Jasmine, acid in every word, "where were you the whole time? Showing up to borrow my clothes for dates and then disappearing. Did you even wash the clothes before returning them? Texting me that Shanice was definitely crazy, but then immediately taking her side? Shanice had some excuse because of the drugs, but you were just a shitty, shitty friend and a leech. Still are."

Before Ash could respond, Shanice spoke. "You told her I was crazy? You told me she was jealous!"

Ash was grimacing with this confrontation. "You *were* being crazy," said Ash rolling her eyes, "and she *is* jealous. The only sane one is me."

"*Stop!*" Michelle burst out. "Can y'all stop bickering for just one minute and try to be my friends again?"

"Sheesh, you must really want that *stupid* apartment," murmured Ash.

Michelle shot daggers out of her eyes. "You think this is about an apartment?" she growled. "You're all so fucking dumb!"

Ashwini went slack-jawed, and Shanice's eyes were the size of saucers. Though hostility was routine in the group dynamic, Michelle never called anyone out. Usually, she was the voice of reason when everyone else went off the deep end. Yet Michelle was calling them out, staring Ash down with a venomous unblinking glare. She looked like a pissed off rattlesnake about to strike.

"Michelle," said Jasmine softly, laying a hand on Michelle's arm, "are you okay?"

Michelle hissed. "I get it. I left, everything changed, and now I'm back, and the world's moved on. But you know what, I didn't. I haven't fucking moved on. I loved our friendship. *Loved it.* Yeah, it wasn't perfect, but it was perfect for me. Hearing about Jas's weird health kicks, Shanice's adventures, and Ash's dating life. That was our groove. We supported one another. Or I thought we did. But I guess none of y'all care about that and would rather tear it down than build us up." Michelle scratched around her face with her hands, leaving red lines behind.

"You know, I never wanted to admit it, but I hated France. I hated it so much. Them and their stupid food and their condescending bullshit. I despised it. Not to mention, it was so fucking lonely. And I just kept thinking, thank God I have somewhere to go back to. People who I belong with. But apparently, while I was gone, that all went to shit. Literally flushed down the toilet. Ash, I didn't throw this brunch to force y'all to move into our literal dream apartment with me, though I did have my hopes. I threw this brunch so I could feel at home again, apartment or no apartment." Michelle dotted the corners of her eyes to remove the formation of tears. "I guess home no longer exists. There's no point for hope." Then Michelle began sobbing. Messy sobbing, with gasps that sounded like children crying for help and tears flowing endlessly down her face.

Jasmine tried to soothe Michelle, whispering soft shushing noises. Shanice got up from her seat to rub at Michelle's other arm. Ash sat frozen in her chair, turned to stone by Michelle's monologue. Around them, the restaurant had gone eerily quiet. A stranger from a nearby table stopped by to give them a crinkled pack of tissues, which Jasmine used to gently dab at Michelle's face. Shanice continued patting Michelle's arm and watched Jasmine dry her friend's tears.

It took a while, but gradually Michelle's sobs went from seal barks to small hiccups. Shanice sat back in her seat. Life in the surrounding tables had already returned to normal. At their table, crumpled tear- and snot-laden tissues covered everything.

At that moment, there was a breeze, and the waitress arrived with Michelle's drink. A delicate white flower adorned the glass containing murky purple liquid.

"Thank goodness," said Michelle in a high-pitched squeak, pretending to be okay for the waitress. "I've needed this for a while."

"I'll take one of those," said Shanice to the waitress, while pointing to her own empty glass.

"Me too," said Ash and began sullenly chugging the remainder of her current drink.

"And you?" asked the waitress to Jasmine.

Jasmine inspected the half glass of yellow concoction she had left before looking around at the table. "I guess I'll have one too," said Jasmine. "We're going to be here for a while."

"Coming up," said the waitress, who shuffled away quickly, forgetting to clear Shanice's empty glass.

"I thought you were limiting alcohol because 'your body is a temple' or something," said Ash after finishing her drink.

"Two drinks are acceptable if I eat a full meal and am with friends," said Jasmine softly. "And I think we should take time to work through this, for Michelle."

Michelle smiled weakly. Her face was swollen from the crying, and she continued to pat at it with the napkin from her lap. They'd run out of the stranger's tissues.

"I agree," said Shanice taking a deep breath. "I'll start. Jas, I don't know if I ever really thanked you for being there when I first got the shot. Watching you comfort Michelle just now brought back some memories. Anyway, I know it was a lot, and I really should have thanked you sooner."

Jasmine nodded slowly.

"I'm sorry I couldn't do more when you needed me," said Jasmine taking off her sunglasses. "And I'm sorry, Shanice and Ashwini. I said some pretty unconstructive criticism earlier."

"Eh, you were right though," said Ash, nursing her empty glass, "I never did wash the clothes you lent me." The group chuckled hesitantly. The sun had shifted so that they were now in pleasant shade.

"I'm glad we're here together today," said Shanice with warmth. Everyone nodded.

"So, Michelle, what do you want to talk about?" asked Ashwini.

"Um, I don't know," said Michelle with unusual uncertainty. "Hey, I'm sorry about the meltdown. I'm about to get my period, and I've been having PMS pretty bad lately."

"No need to apologize!" said Jasmine.

"We all deserved the call out," said Shanice. Ashwini and Jasmine agreed. Everyone looked at Michelle expectantly, waiting for her to say something. Next door, their waitress delivered drinks, avoiding looking at their table.

"New topic, I guess?" asked Michelle. No one spoke. "Um, Has anyone tried period panties? They're surprisingly wonderful. I'm wearing them right now, actually."

"Gross," said Jasmine without hesitation, "I only use all-cotton tampons." Michelle laughed lightly.

"How do they compare to pads?" asked Ashwini with a genuine interest in her voice. Ashwini was firmly in the pad-camp and never wore tampons.

"Ash, they would be perfect for you. They're great," said Michelle. "The brand even makes a swimsuit, which I thought might interest you."

"Seriously?" said Shanice. "I'm with Jas on this one. Menstrual blood and pubic hair don't mix. Though it would be nice not to plan beach days around Ash's cycle. Remember that time freshman year? Her jumbo pad came out in the ocean!"

Everyone but Ash chuckled.

"It was one time! You know I don't swim on my period anymore," said Ash. Then her voice dropped to a notch above a whisper, and she continued, "Also, the whole blood and hair thing isn't a problem if you don't *have* any hair." A thin smile formed on her face, and her eyes twinkled.

"Or you accept that bleeding and pubic hair are both natural processes, but shoving fabric up your vagina is not. Micro-tears are still tears," said Michelle confidently, then looked at Ashwini, who was still smiling suggestively. "Wait, Ash, you don't have pubic hair?"

"Started fully waxing a month ago," said Ash, her excitement bubbling up. "Isaiah really likes it!" Isaiah was Ashwini's boyfriend.

"Ooooooh, girl!" said Shanice. "I've been thinking about that. I shave, but waxing is next level."

"Is it organic?" asked Jasmine.

"I think so," said Ash, "I go to a salon on D street, and with their prices, they better be organic."

The waitress arrived with their food. Plates topped with perfectly cooked eggs, golden pancakes, and spotted with brightly colored melon slices and berries.

"I'm so glad to be back," said Michelle, smile lines forming at her eyes. "Now, time for a group photo with the food? Our tradition?"

"Glad to have you back and of course! Let's use my phone for the photo," said Shanice. "I love its camera."

Michelle and Jasmine got up from their seats and stood behind Shanice and Ashwini. Shanice handed her phone to a nearby waiter. The four all leaned in.

"On the count of three, let's all say 'Fuck France,'" said Shanice. Michelle giggled. "One… two… three…"

"Fuck France!" the four shouted as the waiter clicked the camera.

The restaurant became quiet as people looked toward the source of the noise. All they saw were four friends smiling, laughing, and taking brunch photos.

CHAPTER NINE

NO PAIN NO GAIN?

———

The lubricant had been cold, and the sensation of Doctor Kuznetsov inserting the rod into her vagina was bizarre. Daneen had never had a transvaginal ultrasound before or, for that matter, a male gynecologist. Making things worse, the device's insertion triggered the deep vaginal ache she'd felt for most of the past month. Daneen tried to distract herself by counting the pockmarked ceiling tiles. She'd gotten to a dozen before Doctor Kuznetsov spoke. The words rang in her ears.

"There's no way she could have gotten it in," said Dr. Kuznetsov.

That bitch, thought Daneen.

***

A month ago, Daneen had given up on NuvaRing—the small, flexible vaginal ring used to prevent pregnancy.

Daneen and her boyfriend Kevin had been having sex with Daneen on top. Daneen liked being on top because she had a better sense of pace than Kevin, who was as rhythmically consistent as a Jazz band, and she was in better shape. It was going well until Daneen decided to twist from front-facing cowgirl to backward cowgirl. That's when her NuvaRing decided it wanted out.

With a small squelch, a ring the size of a coaster and the diameter of an earthworm popped onto Kevin's chest.

"Ahhhh!" Kevin had shrieked. Kevin, an avid horror fan, had mistaken the ring on his stomach for some type of snake-like parasite.

Daneen, facing Kevin's feet, brought her hands to her ears as the door burst open.

"Daneen!" shouted Albert, running into the room, almost sliding into the bed. He'd mistaken Kevin's high-pitched yell for his roommate Daneen.

Jumping off of Kevin, Daneen turned like a frightened cat to see Albert's concerned face so close she could have touched it, Kevin's shocked look of horror, and the vaginal-mucus-covered ring heaving up and down on Kevin's stomach.

It was at that moment Daneen decided the NuvaRing was no longer for her.

That night, Daneen told Kevin she wanted to pause sex while she figured out a replacement form of birth control and got a lock for her door. Kevin had readily agreed and offered his help.

***

The following Sunday, Daneen was hanging out at Kevin's tiny one-bedroom apartment for a relaxed afternoon. While he worked from the IKEA desk, which he had bought secondhand, she lay out on his futon under the ancient single-pane window.

"Grrrhhhhh!" growled Daneen, a laptop on her stomach and her head propped up by one of Kevin's sweatshirts she'd smushed into a pillow-shaped lump.

"You okay?" asked Kevin, taking off his massive over-ear headphones. "You broke through my noise cancelation."

"Sorry. I'm just so frustrated." Daneen puffed noisily. "I've spent the last hour on Wikipedia, and I feel even more confused about my birth control options. Did you know the FDA has approved over twenty different pills and a phone app based on thermometer readings? A phone app. Based on thermometer readings! And don't even get me started on this new gel thing! It sounds like spermicide, but apparently, it's not spermicide? Also, does anyone use spermicide? Do they still even make that gunk? *Ughh*, I'm in an information black hole, and it's sucking away my life force."

"Hey, it's okay," said Kevin. "A lot of options is a good thing!" Kevin swiveled his chair and rolled toward Daneen. She smirked, and Kevin continued, "If you want my help sorting through birth controls, you know I'm here and that I love data."

"I know you offered, but are you sure?" asked Daneen. "That wouldn't be taking advantage of you for your massive brain?"

"Are you trying to butter me up?"

"Maybe. I just don't know if I can sort through all of this. I almost wish I hadn't thrown out my NuvaRing," said Daneen, scratching at her elbow.

"You did the right thing. Why don't I do some digging on what's out there while you start dinner? Then we can talk through what you want?"

"You're the best," said Daneen, closing her laptop. She got up and gave Kevin a peck on the cheek.

"I know," said Kevin, smiling.

Kevin, a detail-oriented Masters student, immediately nerded out learning about different forms of birth control. By the time Daneen was done stir-frying their dinner and they began eating, he was pretty confident in his assessment.

"It's incredible that a phone app, Natural Cycles, is over 90 percent effective, but we really should aim for over 98 percent. By that measure, I'm really not impressed with the NuvaRing. With its 91 percent effectiveness, it leaves eight percent of NuvaRing users pregnant in a year. That's a lot! I can't believe we didn't know that," emphasized Kevin while scrolling through the notes on his phone.

"Hmmm, yeah, I didn't realize that. I knew the pill was better, but I switched over to the NuvaRing so I could stop having to remember to take it every day. It was annoying. I guess I'd be okay with turning back on my pill alarm reminder if I have to," said Daneen, getting up to refill her water glass. The memory of Kevin's shriek when the NuvaRing popped out echoed in her ears.

"Unfortunately, I also don't think the pill's a great option," said Kevin. "Sure, if you take it perfectly, it's 99 percent effective, but if you don't take it at the exact same time every day or you skip a pill or two, that effectiveness goes down the toilet. I love you, Daneen, but neither of us is ready for a baby, and pregnancy is surprisingly likely on the pill unless we use a secondary form of birth control. Instead, if you're open to it, I think a hormonal IUD is your best bet, specifically Skyla or Kyleena. And I think Kyleena would work best for your priorities."

While there'd been five IUD options, all over 99 percent effective, Kevin had whittled the list down to avoid overloading Daneen. Kevin had ruled out Paragard (the only nonhormonal IUD) since it was known for making cramping worse, and he knew Daneen wouldn't like that. While cooking, Daneen had also told Kevin she didn't want to lose her period. While some of her friends loved not having a period, Daneen liked knowing her body was working every month. That took off two other hormonal IUDs from the list because they were highly correlated with a loss of period bleeding, leaving Skyla and Kyleena.

"Interesting," said Daneen, poking a steaming snap pea with her fork. "I don't know much about either of them."

"Skyla is the least likely to remove your periods, but it needs replacement every three years. Apparently, the worst part of an IUD is the insertion, so it's better to have an IUD that lasts longer. That takes us to Kyleena. You don't have to worry about it for five years, there's roughly an 80 percent chance you get to keep your period, which I know you want, and it's over 99 percent effective. Plus, it's smaller than some of the other IUDs, so insertion should be easier. And that's everything I've got." Kevin took a big forkful of stir fry, leaning over the miniature dining room table to ensure all the food made it into his mouth.

"Kyleena sounds great. Thanks, Kevin. I hate dealing with medical stuff," said Daneen while twisting a fork in her steaming bowl of noodles, veggies, and tofu.

"I know," Kevin murmured through a mouth still full of food, "glad to help."

Daneen wasn't sure it was normal to have a boyfriend so involved in birth control products, but she liked Kevin's tenacious problem-solving. She'd once lost an earring, and he'd searched for it for over an hour before finding it had fallen into a crumpled tissue in the trash. She hadn't even liked the earring that much, but she loved how Kevin had searched for it.

***

The next week Kevin drove Daneen to the doctor's office and sat in the waiting room with her. The room was off-white and had a small fish tank with a gulping goldfish. Daneen crossed, uncrossed, and recrossed her legs restlessly, anxious about her upcoming IUD insertion with Nurse Florian. Kevin gave her hand two squeezes, like a heartbeat. Daneen began tapping her foot in the air.

"Daneen?" said Nurse Florian, entering the waiting room in scrubs.

"Good luck, babe," said Kevin giving Daneen's hand another two quick squeezes. His hand was warm in the chilly office's AC breeze.

"Hello Daneen, I'm Nurse Florian, come with me," said the nurse, then turned to Kevin. "She'll be out in less than fifteen minutes."

Nurse Florian led Daneen to the examination room. The room had an eerie absence of smell. "FOR NEEDLES ONLY" written in bright red on the hazardous waste box was the only real color in the room. Everything else was white, beige, or gray. Even the view out the window was gray and cloudy. Nurse Florian gestured for Daneen to sit on the beige chair across from the gray and beige bed stirrup contraption.

"So, Daneen, we're here today for a Kyleena IUD insertion. I've gotten your pregnancy test results back, and they are negative, so we're ready to go. Do you have any questions before we get started?" said Nurse Florian

"Will it hurt?" asked Daneen.

"A bit, but you should be fine in a couple of hours. It's a very simple procedure," said Nurse Florian and then handed Daneen a generic blue hospital gown. "Okay, I'll step out for a minute. While I'm gone, please remove your pants, underwear, and shoes, and put on the gown. You're free to leave on your top, bra, and socks." The nurse stepped out, and Daneen stripped off her bottoms, leaving them in a crumpled pile on the white windowsill. She put on the gown. Soon the nurse was back in, and Daneen was in the stirrups.

"It'll only be a pinch," said Nurse Florian.

Daneen felt the pinch of the speculum, but it didn't bother her too much. Then sudden pain shot through her body like electricity, a small explosion tearing at her from inside her vagina.

"Ow!" Daneen yelped.

"Please stay still," said Nurse Florian, "we're almost done."

Daneen tried to stay still, closing her eyes to focus, but the pain struck again.

"Uh!" Daneen cried through closed lips. The pain felt like a laser burning through Daneen's groin.

"I'm so close, but I need you to stop moving," said Nurse Florian. As the pain began to fade slightly, Daneen clenched every muscle in her body, willing them to stay still.

Ten, nine, eight. Daneen tried in vain to count in her head as a distraction from the waves of pain.

"Oooowwww!" burst Daneen. The world went black, and all that existed was suffering. Daneen squirmed and writhed, pushing against the stirrups and the table. It was like nothing she'd ever felt before, like burning coals shoved up her vagina.

"If you don't stop, I can't get this in, and I always get them in!" said Nurse Florian, practically yelling into Daneen's groin.

At this point, Daneen was moaning and shaking on the table. One more wave of pain was all she could handle.

"Stop!" Daneen screamed. It was the only word she could manage between shallow breaths.

"Fine, but stop yelling," said Nurse Florian shaking her head. "It's not in, but that's not my fault. You wouldn't stop moving. I've never seen anything so dramatic. Over a dozen insertions, and I've never had an issue." Nurse Florian removed the speculum. "Don't come back unless you take the ibuprofen ahead of time as you were instructed to before this visit. I'm leaving. Put your clothes back on and then head to the front desk."

Nurse Florian shut the door behind her. It closed with a loud thud.

Daneen lay on the table and grasped at consciousness, and tried to regain her breath. After a couple of minutes, she started to feel human again. The pain, a stinging ache deep in her vagina, continued.

But I did take the ibuprofen, thought Daneen, her head still foggy with pain.

Removing her feet from the stirrups, Daneen pushed herself up into a sitting position. She held herself, gripping the gown to her stomach, trying not to barf from the agony.

It took her almost half an hour to get up, change, and head to the waiting room, where Kevin sat anxiously. Twice someone had knocked on the door of the exam room, and she'd had to say she was still inside. As Daneen finally hobbled into the waiting room, Kevin jumped from his chair and rushed over to her.

"Talk in the car," she whispered and then leaned on him. Kevin was silent as he helped her out to the car. He stood at her door.

"You're white as a ghost," said Kevin, caressing her cheek delicately, "a Casper-style ghost. What happened? You were gone for an hour!"

"Please turn on the car," said Daneen ashen-faced, "I need the heated seat. Daneen tried to describe the pain on the way home as Kevin drove and bit his lip in concentration.

***

A month later, Doctor Kuznetsov performed an ultrasound, and Daneen found out what really had happened. After Daneen, still pale, had told Kevin she'd left the exam room without an IUD, he'd taken it as a personal failing. He'd then called all the highest-rated gynecologists in the area. Doctor Kuznetsov had the first opening, and Kevin had found a substitute for the office hours he hosted for undergraduates in order to drive Daneen to the appointment.

Based on her recollection of the IUD insertion attempt, Doctor Kuznetsov had scheduled Daneen for a transvaginal ultrasound. Daneen tried to disregard the fact Doctor Kuznetsov was a man, but upon meeting him, his large eyebrows and Santa beard were hard to ignore, making Daneen increasingly nervous. Very few men had seen Daneen's vagina, and now Doctor Kuznetsov would be on that short list. When he shook her hand with his large mitt, she thought, *that hand is too big for my vagina.* But Kevin had made almost a dozen phone calls to get this appointment, and she knew deep down something was wrong, so she'd duly changed into another hospital gown and put her feet in this new set of stirrups. *Plus,* she reminded herself, *the sooner this is over, the sooner I can have sex again.*

The lubricant on Daneen's vulva was fluid as the doctor directed the ultrasound rod into Daneen's vagina. The insertion triggered the vaginal ache she'd felt for most of the past month. Doctor Kuznetsov took a minute to look around, angling the rod from left to right and up and down, inspecting the resulting images on a black and white screen.

"So, Daneen," said Doctor Kuznetsov, his voice warm in the chilly room, "you have a tilted uterus. It also looks like that nurse punctured your vaginal wall multiple times, attempting to insert the IUD. She must have been very determined to have done this much damage, but there's no way she could have gotten it in," said Dr. Kuznetsov.

That bitch, thought Daneen. "Good to know," she said aloud.

"Your vaginal wall is healing, but if you're still interested in an IUD, I'd recommend we wait a couple of weeks before a proper insertion. We'd have an ultrasound running during the process to ensure correct IUD placement and to minimize issues," said Doctor Kuznetsov.

The words gently washed over Daneen.

"I'm going to remove the ultrasound rod now." Doctor Kuznetsov gently pulled the device out. It slid with ease, and Daneen's soreness began to fade the minute it was out.

"Thank you," said Daneen.

"No need to thank me," said Doctor Kuznetsov, "just doing my job. Tell that nervous nelly of a boyfriend that you're going to be fine. Having a tilted uterus is normal. One in five women have them. Other than difficulty inserting an IUD and potential back pain during pregnancy, it shouldn't cause you any issues. Now, do you have any questions or concerns?"

"Yes, what about a tilted uterus makes it difficult? Could the IUD puncture me coming out?" Daneen shivered at the thought, remembering the pain of the first attempted insertion.

"Great question! The IUD is actually flexible and won't have any issue with the tilt. The problem with insertion is that the standard tool used to insert the IUD isn't flexible. Therefore, during insertion navigating the IUD around a curve is difficult. But once it's in, pulling an IUD out is easy and extremely low risk. What other questions do you have?"

"None, actually. I feel a lot better," said Daneen, and she did. The room didn't feel quite as cold now, and the knot in her stomach had unclenched.

"Glad to hear it. It was a pleasure meeting you, Daneen. I'm going to leave the room, so take your time to clean up and then head to the front desk. There's a bathroom attached to this room for your convenience. If you have any more questions, please don't hesitate to call."

"Will do," said Daneen.

As Doctor Kuznetsov shut the door gently behind him, Daneen rubbed her stomach and took in the room. On the wall, there was a picture of a happy bunny munching on a carrot. Kevin had told her about the bunny before the appointment. While Kevin was reading through all of Doctor Kuznetsov's reviews, one of the many five-star comments had mentioned the chubby bunny. Daneen decided to take a picture and text it to Kevin with the caption, "I'm okay."

When I get home, I'm going to have a piece of cake, thought Daneen. *After all this, I deserve it.*

CHAPTER TEN

MORE PAIN

———

I was taking a break playing Fortnite when my phone buzzed in my back pocket. I thought about ignoring the call, but I knew from experience that it wouldn't work. She'd call and call again, and when I finally did answer, it would be a mind-numbing earful of, "Oh Aakil, my son, I was so worried!" or "Oh Aakil, I was about to call the police!" My mom is so overbearing. A loving person, but a total headache. She once called campus security to check on me when I didn't call her back for a couple of days. I'm in college. I'm busy. I've thought about telling her to get her meds checked but decided it wasn't worth the drama. Once I'm a doctor, I definitely will, though.

I picked up the phone and said, "Yes, Mom?" Immediately her voice crackled through on the other end of the line.

"Aakil, have you talked with your sister Hiral?" Mom said. Great, my least favorite topic.

Just because Hiral is my twin sister and we happen to go to the same college does not make us friends. I don't even know how she got in here. I had a 3.8 GPA in high school and volunteered at a senior living facility. All she did was play volleyball. And she's not even on the volleyball team anymore.

Hiral started complaining to Mom about horrific shin splints the moment she moved into her dorm, then dropped off the team less than two months into the season. Apparently, horrific shin splints stopped her from playing volleyball but in no way prevented her from dancing at fraternity parties every night. I've seen the videos, and I'm not an idiot. Hiral is a quitter and a dramatic liar. Even so, I tried that whole, 'let's make amends and be friends' thing freshman year. It was going okay until Hiral refused to set me up with her friend. It might've been fine, but she kept making dumb excuses that made no sense.

"No, Mom, I don't talk with Hiral," I said on the phone, my voice flat. I began to twirl the Coors Light on the wood veneer of the desk, forming a circle. A lot of people don't like Coors Light, but I actually think it's a solid beer. Not too strong, so perfect to drink while studying. The many circular stains on the desk attested to this fact.

"Oh, Aakil, that's silly." Mom's always been in denial about how disingenuous Hiral is. "Offer to bring her some food when you talk to her. She's been vomiting all day." Vomiting all day, and no one asked me for advice? I literally volunteer as an EMT sixteen hours a week, and Mom treats me like I'm a little boy playing dress-up. Last week I did chest compressions on a fifteen-year-old kid for over ten minutes.

Had anyone bothered to ask me about Hiral's condition, I would have told them vomiting that much sounds like food poisoning or pregnancy. But they didn't ask. Of course, Hiral would get knocked up before finishing college. At this rate, I'm going to make an excellent doctor, and she's going to make an excellent nothing. I know that's harsh, but I'm so sick of her shit. I bet "vomiting all day" really means Hiral vomited once and then bitched about it to Mom for two hours on the phone.

"Sure, Mom," I said, looking at the bright light of Fortnite on my computer screen. The light bounced off an empty bag of chips. I needed more chips. "I have to get back to studying, and I have an EMT shift early tomorrow."

"Okay, Babu, I love you."

"Bye, Mom, don't forget to take the vitamins I got you," I said and hung up the phone. I'd gotten Mom some magnesium pills after she'd mentioned being more tired than normal. Her regular doctor is useless, so I make sure she's taken care of.

I wouldn't have thought about that conversation, but the next day my mom called again. I say the next day, but honestly, it could have been an hour later—I was drinking a Coors Light, playing Fortnite, and it was twilight outside. The same pile of chemistry books lay on the ground by my bed, and the same crumpled pile of laundry sat in the corner. (My mom had offered to wash it for me when I came home, a three-hour drive, and I didn't want to offend her).

"Yes, Mom?" I said, picking up the phone and putting it on speaker. I tried not to sound annoyed, not that Mom would notice. She's oblivious to all social cues.

"Oh, Aakil, I need you to drive to the medical center and pick up your sister. I've told her you're coming," said Mom. This was an unusual request, but I wasn't in the mood to ask questions.

"Mom, I'm studying." I grabbed a chip from the new bag on the desk and began to munch.

"What's that crunching?" said Mom.

"Study snack," I said, examining the back of the bag of chips. Once I'm a doctor, I won't be allowed to eat chips anymore, too much saturated fat, so I'm making sure to get my fill before medical school.

"Aakil, I'm sorry you're going to have to pause studying. You need to get your sister and drive her to her dorm."

"Why can't she walk?" I said, knowing Hiral lived a good twenty minutes away from the medical center, but I was mid-drink, and I usually avoided driving if I'd had any alcohol. Better safe than sorry. Plus, Mom was always asking me to do things for Hiral that neither of us wanted, like the time she tried to make me tutor Hiral in Calculus. "Or take the shuttle?"

I hated the shuttles. They always smelled like stale beer, never came on time, and somehow took over an hour to get you somewhere you could walk to in ten minutes. That's why I'd told my parents they had to buy me a car sophomore year. They did, but they made me promise to drive Hiral to and from school for all the holidays, so I'd paid the cost many times over.

"She's sick," said Mom, unusually curt. "Aakil, you need to go pick her up and make sure she gets to her dorm okay. Daddy and I will be coming down tomorrow if you're free for dinner, but if you're too busy with your studies, we understand."

That sentence set off alarm bells in my head. Mom and Dad had only ever come to campus once to drop us off freshman year. Dad complained the whole way about his arthritis, and Mom had a tizzy about highway accidents. After that, they'd made us take a smelly Greyhound to and from school freshman year. Then, before our sophomore year, they bought me my car. They hadn't come when I'd made the Dean's List or even once for one of Hiral's volleyball games before she quit, and they'd gone to every one of her games in high school. Hiral must be more ill than I thought.

"Uhh," I said, deciding if I was safe to drive. Picking up the can, I clocked that it was only half-empty.

"So you're on your way to get your sister?" said Mom.

"Yeah," I said.

"Thanks, Babu. I love you," said Mom.

"Bye," I said and hung up.

The drive was dark, even though it was barely 5 p.m. Snow fell lazily to the ground, forming gray piles on the sides of the road like cigarette ash. The drive was around five minutes, but I took my time stopping fully at the yield signs. Again, better safe than sorry. Also, I wasn't going to rush on Hiral's account. If she was really sick, they'd have her admitted to the hospital. She'd been admitted plenty of times in the past. Pulling up to the imposing brick medical center, I saw it was deserted, no Hiral waiting outside. Typical. When she finally came out of the automatic glass doors, she moved slowly.

"So, how was getting your stomach pumped?" I joked as Hiral got into my car. I almost regretted it when I looked at her collapsed in the seat next to me. Her face was gray, and the circles under her eyes looked like inkwells. "Woof, you look rough."

"Thanks. Let's go," said Hiral, staring blankly out the bug-splattered front window of my car.

"Wait a second, don't I get to know what's going on?" I asked. It was so Hiral to make me drive all the way here and not give me any information. I was curious. I've seen my fair share of sick people, and Hiral looked pretty bad.

"You don't want to know." Hiral continued to stare straight ahead at the untouched snow. Not a lie, but not an answer either. The heaters blasted, and the car hummed. I turned off the engine. Everything went silent, the outside noise muted by the falling snow.

"Try me. I'm pre-med," I said.

"Aakil, I don't want to talk about it," said Hiral, not looking me in the eyes.

"Oh God, did you get an abortion?" I'd always known my sister was promiscuous, but I'd never seriously imagined she'd get pregnant. "Do Mom and Dad know? They're going to disown you." The words came out of my mouth before I could think them through. We couldn't tell my parents. It would be a disaster.

"No, asshole, I didn't have an abortion," said Hiral, irritated. I inspected her. She was rubbing her temples with both hands, which were just as ashen as her face. Her lips looked dry. Her hair was in a greasy unwashed bun. There was even a mild smell of vomit emanating from her. I hadn't seen her this ill in a long time.

"Hiral, don't lie to me. If you got an abortion, it can stay between us two. The parents don't need to know. Dad doesn't need to know. It's better for everyone," I said, subconsciously switching to my 'ambulance tone,' the one I use to reassure particularly disoriented patients. Patients lie or omit details all the time, and it was my job as an EMT to get the most complete and accurate picture so we could make informed medical decisions. Right now, Hiral wasn't my sister. She was a patient who wasn't telling me what I needed to know in order to help her.

Snow continued to fall on the car, and with the heat off the temperature was dropping. Hiral looked toward me, her eyes bloodshot, and shivered.

"Fine, Aakil, if you must know, I've had keyhole vision, vomiting, and trouble walking for two days now. Earlier today, I was diagnosed with something called IIH, though I can't remember what it stands for because I haven't slept in forty-eight hours. After this delightful diagnosis, they had to immediately remove the IUD from my vagina, so my head doesn't explode. Now can you stop being a self-righteous ass, turn the goddamn heat on, and put the car in gear." She paused after this finale, but I didn't respond. I curled my toes and took in a deep breath of the cool air as I began to dissect this communication. Before I'd had time to finish processing, Hiral was talking again. "God, it smells in here. You treat this car like it's a trash can. I told the parents not to buy you a car and that I'd rather keep taking that awful Greyhound bus, but they spoil you. Stop being an unappreciative brat and take me home. Why did you even come? I told Mom not to call you."

"Me unappreciative? You're so selfish, you're ruining everything with your drama, and I'm the only one trying to fix things! Can't you even go a couple of years without ending up in a hospital bed? Do you want to bankrupt our parents? Do you want Mom to have a second heart attack?" All the words, both Hiral's and my own, were rattling around in my head like Boggle cubes. *Keyhole vision? Selfish? IIH? Bankrupt? Head explode?*

"Are you serious right now?" said Hiral, but I couldn't even look at her. I was so angry my face burned, and on my lap sat two clenched fists.

"You heard me!" my voice exploded in the car. "You're killing our parents! Why can't you just leave them alone?"

"What do you want me to do? Die?" Hiral yelled back.

"I don't know," I shouted, the words amplified by the small space. "I don't know," I said again, this time one decibel below a shout. "Why don't you ever ask me for help? Why is

it always Mom's problem? I literally work in an ambulance."
I tried to remember what Hiral had said that was relevant to
a diagnosis. I tried to divorce myself from our relationship
and see her as a patient. It wasn't working.

"So you can judge me?" said Hiral.

"I am not judgmental," I said.

"You just accused me of having an abortion. How is that
not judgmental?" We sat in silence for a minute. The icy white
snow accumulation on the windows felt like being buried
alive. "Aakil, I don't know what you're issue is, but I don't
have the energy for this. Please, just turn the heat on and
drive me home. I don't feel well."

My face was hot, and my ears burned. I turned the car
on and let it idle. The seat underneath me began to rumble.
It felt like I was underwater during an earthquake.

I searched my mind for a distraction, anything to get
my head out of this car. Instantly I saw the fifteen-year-old
kid I had given chest compressions. His green collared shirt
and the snap of his lifeless ribs under my palms. Somewhere
nearby, sounds of a child gasping for air between quiet sobs.
His little sister? My eyes burned, but I needed to keep going.
I needed to save their family. This was not the distraction I
wanted. This was worse than Hiral's loathing. The memory
burned. I brought my mind back into the car.

"I don't treat this car like a garbage can," I argued under
my breath. Why was this so different than being in the ambulance? Usually, I was so calm, even when the patient was
wailing or crying. I needed to get back in control.

"Fine, you treat this car like a queen," said Hiral, kick-
ing at some chip wrappers at her feet. They crinkled. "Now,
please drive me home, or should I just walk? I might fall

over a couple of times, but it'll be more pleasant than this conversation." Then under her breath, she added, "Asshole."

I turned on the defrost vents and ran the window wipers to clear off the snow, boxing us in. A rush of air blew through the car, and the tires crunched snow as I pulled out of the parking lot. We didn't talk.

I thought about all the times Hiral had gone to the hospital. The first time was when we were thirteen. No one ever told me why, but Hiral had clearly been anorexic. Mom canceled our spring break cruise, and instead, I spent break at home alone. My friends all thought I was on the cruise, and I didn't want to have to explain why I wasn't. My parents were almost always at the hospital, but I hated being there. I could still see thirteen-year-old Hiral lying in the hospital bed, eerily thin and her face covered in peach fuzz. I'm pretty sure she almost died. By saving Hiral, her doctors not only saved my sister, they also saved my entire family. Since then, I've wanted to be a doctor and give hope to families like mine. Now I love going to the hospital. It gives me a sense of purpose like I can make a difference. But back then, I felt so lonely and helpless, angry at my sister for being sick. It's funny how some things change, and some things don't.

The drive was short. Somehow it had gotten even darker outside while we drove. The moon and a single star twinkled faintly above.

I pulled up in front of Hiral's dorm, an older building made of concrete that looked like a Soviet-era bunker, and shifted the car to park. A good thirty feet stood between us and the front door, and I knew the walk to Hiral's dorm included a flight of stairs. Hiral unbuckled her seatbelt.

"Hiral," I said gingerly. She turned her head. Everyone has always said for fraternal twins that we don't look much alike, except for our eyes, and locking eyes with her tonight was like looking into a mirror. I shuddered, and she glowered in response.

"I'm sorry for being a jerk," I said. "Can I help you get to your room?"

Hiral stared at me, and I noticed while one hand was on the door, the other gripped her stomach protectively. She was still in pain.

"What's the catch?" said Hiral. "My roommate's not interested in you."

"No catch, I just want to make sure you get to bed okay," I said. The space between us was gently glowing with moonlight.

"Fine, but this doesn't mean you're not an asshole," said Hiral flatly.

"Sure," I said. Without meaning to, the word came out almost sarcastic. I bit my tongue and turned off the car, getting out and walking to Hiral's door. As she got out, I offered her the crook of my elbow. She held it tentatively at first but tighter as we began to walk across the slick sidewalk.

We slowly shuffled toward the heavy front door in silence. I maneuvered the door open with my free hand.

As we pattered gradually to the worn stairwell, Hiral took one step at a time. It hurt to see her so weak and in pain. It was like stepping back in time, but I swallowed the feeling and helped her soundlessly.

When we got to her room, she handed me the cold metal key. The room was empty, though photos of Hiral and her many friends smiled at us from the walls. I helped this frail grimacing version of my sister to her bed, where she sat down.

"I'm glad you're okay," I said. "Can I get you anything? Gatorade? Crackers?" The room was uncomfortably warm and dry.

"No," said Hiral with certainty. "You can go now."

"Please let me help you," I said gently. "I know I've been a shitty brother historically, but I'm a damn good EMT."

Hiral's eyes were closed, and she looked almost asleep as she said, "Fine, orange Gatorade and crackers."

I left, heading to the convenience store next door. The store was cramped but overflowing with snack food. I got two bottles of orange Gatorade, a box of saltines, a couple of Kind bars, and a bag of sour gummy worms. The gummies were an impulse purchase. When I saw them, they reminded me of when we were kids. On road trips, Hiral and I used to split a bag of gummy worms and have the worm kingdoms attack each other. That was until Hiral stopped eating sugar.

When I got back to Hiral's room, I knocked on the hollow door. No answer, but I went in. The lights were on, and Hiral was lying on the bed corpselike. My throat caught.

"Oh, you're back," croaked Hiral opening her eyes, "I was napping." She sat up on her bed.

"Oh," I said, pushing away the thoughts of death. "Orange Gatorade, crackers, some protein bars in case you don't want to get out of bed for a day, and some sour gummy worms." I thrust the bag toward her.

"Thanks," she said. I stood there as she looked in the bag. She took the gummy worms out. For a second, I thought she was going to tell me to take them away. Maybe she wasn't eating sugar again, but then she surprised me.

"I haven't had these in forever," said Hiral while tearing open the plastic bag. "Want one?" The sugary smell wafted toward me and reminded me of simpler times.

"Sure," I said. Hiral held out the bag, and I grabbed a gummy. It had an electric blue head and an orange tail. I didn't eat it quite yet. "Hiral, seeing you sick is really hard. It's always been hard. Anyway, I know I said some stupid shit earlier, and I didn't mean it."

"Thanks, I guess," said Hiral, munching on a cherry red and sunshine yellow worm.

"I'm not always the best with people, but I am working on it." I stood there and, after a moment, Hiral gestured for me to sit in the chair by her desk. I chewed on my gummy worm. It was sour and sweet, exactly like I remembered. I finished it quickly, and Hiral offered me the bag again.

"I know it wasn't easy growing up with me as a twin sister," said Hiral, "I just wish you'd cut me slack sometimes. Until this week, I hadn't been to the hospital in over two years. I've never wanted to be sick. It sucks."

"I see that now. You look like shit. Sorry, I meant to say you look rough. Working in the ambulance has shown me how hard it is to be sick and that people don't choose to be ill. I used to think otherwise." I chewed another worm and swallowed. "So, can I ask why your head might explode?"

"I guess, as long as you don't go mental again," said Hiral, "I could use an opportunity to vent." She watched as I nodded, then turned her head away as if speaking to the ceiling. "I don't remember much of what the doctor said, but apparently, I have a rare condition where my brain pressure's messed up. He listed a bunch of things to avoid, so my head doesn't explode, including something about flying on planes that was totally unclear. What was clear is I'm definitely not allowed to be on any hormonal birth control ever again. It's really annoying, actually. My period is very irregular, and birth control was the one thing that helped. The human body is so bizarre and annoying. My brain's fucked, so now drugs for my ovaries could kill me. Plus, the doctor told me losing weight might help reduce symptoms, which is just not something I needed to hear. Asshole. Anyway, that was all probably way too much information to tell my brother, but you're into health stuff, so…" her words trailed off.

I sat digesting this information, unsure how to respond. All I managed to get out was, "Wow."

"I've made the pre-med speechless," said Hiral, laughing to herself. Then she yawned, which made me yawn. Hiral chuckled again. "Twins."

"Twins," I responded. On the desk next to me sat a notebook full of Hiral's bubbly handwriting organized into distinct bullet points, notes for one of her classes. "Sounds like we should both get some rest. Dinner with Dad and Mom tomorrow?" I asked softly. Around me, the many photos of Hiral full of joy smiled at me.

"Yeah," said the real Hiral taking a sip of the Gatorade. "Maybe after you can show them the ambulance you work in. They're really proud of you, you know?"

"Yeah," I said, "They really care about both of us." I got up to leave.

"Thanks for coming," said Hiral.

Without realizing it, I was smiling at her. Quickly, I brought my face back to neutral. "You're going to be okay," I said. "Want me to turn the lights off?"

"Yeah," said Hiral.

"Call me if you need anything." I turned off the lights and went back to my dorm.

In my room, the remaining Coors Lite was warm, but I drank it as I went on WebMD for Idiopathic Intracranial Hypertension, also known as IIH.

CHAPTER ELEVEN

BLOOD BLUES

—

Be eleven. Read about the British monarchy and hemophilia. You know you don't have hemophilia, but you worry about it constantly. You dream the blood is draining from your body through a small cut drop by drop. When your period arrives, feel the rush through your vagina and panic that all your blood is going to empty out of your body one menstrual cycle at a time. Analyze how much blood is on every pair of underwear. Tell your cousin your deepest fear. Your cousin laughs at you loudly, like a cartoon King Henry VIII would after Anne Boleyn was beheaded.

Be fourteen. Try masturbating. Immediately drink a glass of water afterward to replace any lost fluids. Turns out you love masturbating. Turns out you love masturbating so much you set up a masturbation cave in your closet replete with a cupcake-shaped pillow from Hot Topic, a blanket your grandmother knitted for you, glow stars, a picture of Prince Philippos (of Denmark and Greece), and a green Nalgene water bottle. Always drink a full water bottle after masturbating. Use incognito browsers to read articles on how King Christian VII of Denmark masturbated so much he basically stopped being King. Turns out King Christian VII was mentally ill. Are you mentally ill? Never masturbate on your period. Worry that masturbating on your period will increase blood loss, and you'll need an IV blood transfusion. Don't tell anyone these fears. Don't tell anyone about masturbating.

Be sixteen. Get your driver's permit. Go for your driver's test. Wait your turn in a room which smells like overheated fax machines as your mother pesters you to "smile more or you'll fail your driving test—no one likes a frowning young lady." If Queen Elizabeth II of the UK could drive, so can you. Get in the small car with the driving tester. Attempt to smile, and run over something with a thudding bump. The driving tester tells you to pull over. See the dead possum bleeding out in the road like Quintillus, the Roman emperor. Quintillus bled to death. Vomit. Sing "London Bridge is Falling Down" under your breath to distract yourself from thoughts of exsanguination. You fail your driver's test.

Tell your mom you've been asked to retake the driver's test at a later date. Tell mom you were disqualified because you had to pull over to vomit. Suggest that maybe you have food poisoning. Don't mention the possum or its bloody guts smeared across the road like butter on toast. Get home. Mom hands you a glass of water and says, "drink water and cheer up—you'll live." Take a hot bath to calm your nerves. Try to masturbate, but you're suddenly distracted by thoughts of Seneca the Younger bleeding to death in a bathtub. Seneca the Younger thought the bath would help his blood come out faster. Jump out of the bath like it's filled with burning poison. Drink three cups of cold water. Curl up in your grandma's knitted blanket and watch the history channel.

Be seventeen. Become sexually active. Have sex on wet grass and sandpaper tennis courts. Bring your water bottle with you everywhere. Avoid your boyfriend during your period by saying you need to babysit your kid brother. Your boyfriend suspects nothing. He goes out with friends shooting fireworks from empty school parking lots while you edit his Global Studies paper replacing "Columbia" with "Colombia" and "they're" with "their." Things are going really well. "Mutually" break up with your boyfriend because he's going to Africa for the summer. Tell your friends his rich grandparents paying for him to volunteer in Africa is a form of modern-day colonialism. Change his contact information in your phone to "Loser Leopold."

Dream vividly about sex with your ex-boyfriend. Wait for your period to be over. Your period is taking too long. Watch *The Prince and Me* on your laptop. Masturbate. This is the first time you've masturbated on your period. Gag on the smell of blood. Freak out that your hand is bloody. Wash your hands fervently while quoting Lady Macbeth. Inspect your bed. It's clean. Masturbating on your period isn't as bad as you thought it would be. Restart masturbating. Finish. Chug and refill your bottle of water four times. Blood is 90 percent water, so even if you did lose some blood, the water should replenish it.

Be twenty. Experience independence. Date on and off with boys whose middle names you never learn. Sleep with a man who looks like a young Joseph Stalin, tastes like cigarettes, and is gone in the morning. Love sex. But never on your period. On your period, you masturbate. Not that your period comes much anymore. Since you started birth control last year, free from the health center, your ovaries keep skipping months. Get excited when the red flower occasionally blooms. When it comes, the climax is better. Drink a lot of water. Love yourself every day. Skip class to love yourself. Stay in bed for a month. Stop loving yourself. Something's wrong. Everything's wrong. Then one day, you feel okay again. Emerge from this derelict cocoon and desperately attempt to save your grades from crash landing. Tell anyone who asks that you had mono. You never went to the health center to get tested for mono, but what else could have been wrong with you? Google "meditation" and "self-help for a twenty-year-old" in incognito mode. Pass the semester by a hair.

Be twenty-two. Faint at a Halloween party after being splattered with gooey fake blood. Narrowly avoid being sent to the hospital in an ambulance by claiming you're "totally fine, just dehydrated." You are not dehydrated. Uber home and get in the shower fully clothed. Exit the shower. Make your first therapy appointment. If Princess Diana could speak openly about her mental health issues, so can you. You've wanted to talk to someone for a long time now. Tentatively ask your mom about insurance coverage. Your mom says therapists are "for the weak" and that "you are not weak." Plus, "insurance won't cover the appointment." Drive cautiously to the therapist. Park. Sit in your car and stare at the black tar of the road. Ignore your aggressively vibrating cell phone. Drive home. Delete the therapist's voicemail. Have a glass of herbal tea. Get in bed. Masturbate. Decide that you feel better. Decide to stay in for Halloween next year.

Be twenty-four. Date long distance. Why did your boyfriend have to get such a good job so far away? Get familiar with Greyhound buses and their recycled air. As you situate yourself in the polyester seat, you try to make yourself unapproachable, but someone sits right next to you. They're about your age, wearing headphones. Thank God they never speak. Go to the bus's bathroom. Regret this choice. The bathroom smells like piss and is smaller than King Tut's coffin. Change your tampon. Arrive in gleaming Washington DC and feel the historical weight of the city. Prince Constantin and Princess Laurentien of the Netherlands also visited DC recently, and the connection makes you feel like royalty. Immediately offer your boyfriend a blow job. Hope he doesn't notice you're avoiding having sex on your period. It works this trip, but not the next. Tell your boyfriend you've never been with anyone on your period. Tell him you're squeamish. Don't tell him your longstanding fear of a slow, excruciating death via fluid loss. Offer him conciliatory blow jobs. He says he doesn't care about the sex, and as you hug him, he smells like cinnamon and fresh laundry. You give him a blow job anyway. As he sleeps next to you, you toss and turn. Why are you still riddled with this childhood terror?

Be twenty-six. Move in with your fiancé. After four years together, most of it long distance, you love the taste of his morning breath. On Valentine's Day, you get your period. After splitting a bottle of wine, you have sex. It's amazing. Drunk and wet and beautiful. You wake up to bloody sheets. Your own body is flecked with dried blood. Your fiancé is gone to his Saturday morning cleaning at the dentist. You run to the bathroom and throw up in the toilet. Chug water and then throw up again. Chug more water. Tear the sheets off the bed and throw them in a garbage bag. Take a shower. Dispose of the garbage bag. The blood is gone, but you still feel death lingering around you. You drive to T.J. Maxx and buy new sheets. By the time your fiancé comes home, mouth full of fluoride, the new sheets are in the washer. He thanks you for cleaning up with a gentle hello kiss and hopes the sheets won't come out stained. You don't mention the sheets in the washer are new. He suggests next time you put down a towel. You shudder at the thought. "Never again," you whisper to yourself.

Be twenty-seven. Buy a pack of fourteen single-use menstrual discs in preparation for your honeymoon. You've done your research, and this is the best hope for safe, blood-free period sex. You *know* in your brain that period sex is okay, but the message hasn't gotten through to your soul. The idea is that not seeing the blood will trick your soul into compliance. You're going to be fine. You've been doing a lot of yoga, and the meditation has helped with your inner peace. Hopefully, you won't even need the menstrual discs, but better to be cautious.

On your next period, you insert a disk in a trial run. Go about your day and feel liberated. No blood, no spotting, no mentally tallying the fluid lost so far. Your partner notices your good mood and kisses you. His clean-shaven face is soft, and he tastes like warm apple cider. Who can think about death with a man so alive? You continue kissing, and things are going well until he inserts and then pulls out immediately. He can feel something in your vagina. You weren't expecting him to be able to feel it. You blush. You tell him you're not sure what he's talking about. He thinks something is seriously wrong. He's very worried, trotting about like a lively horse. You give in and tell him about the disc. He relaxes. Intimacy is long-dead and forgotten.

Take out the menstrual disc. There isn't as much blood, only maybe a tablespoon, and you pour it slowly in the toilet. Drink a glass of water and then hop in the shower. The waterfall relaxes your tense muscles. Your fiancé asks to join. Your fiancé begins to kiss you under the pounding water. Intimacy has risen from its death like a zombie. You consider objecting, but the idea of giving a blow job in the shower is confusing and unappealing. Have sex in the shower, your foot on the bathtub spout, and your head in the waterfall. It is incredible, an explosion of pleasure.

Be twenty-nine. It's time to make a baby. Stop taking birth control and buy one of those baby naming books. Your husband likes the name Leo, but you veto it. Tell him everyone knows King Leopold was responsible for one of the worst genocides in African history. Cyrus is a much better name for a boy. It doesn't matter, though. You're only going to have girls. Your ovaries took a while to come back to a regular schedule, but your period now comes every twenty-nine days on the mark. Every month it's a disappointment, but at least you get to have well-lubricated shower sex. Exposure has made you a lot more comfortable with blood since it's only momentarily there before it washes down the drain. Subsequently, your husband always makes you a warm cup of pink raspberry tea.

Your husband suggests a couple's therapy package. Trying has been hard on him, harder on you. He says, "What's there to lose? It can only make us a stronger team." You anxiously agree. After a few visits to the office full of prickly cacti and succulent green plants, the therapist asks if you and only you are open to adding in one-on-ones. You've both been making progress in the group sessions, but the therapist senses you have more to talk about. You're hesitant. What if you unravel to this stranger? Will you be able to put yourself back together? Your husband encourages you to, "Go for it! It'll be great." You agree to a one-on-one trial session and remember years ago when you first made a therapy appointment. This time, you plan on showing up.

You give one-on-one therapy a try for the first time. The therapist listens to you with an occasional coo, as if you are a two-legged dog. Soon your face is wet, and you're talking about the bloody possum smeared across the road when you were sixteen. You talk about death, blood, obsession. You're definitely crying now, heavily, but as you speak, you feel physically lighter. After months of one-on-ones, you still hate blood, but when blood gets on a towel, you don't throw it away. Instead, cut the towel into cleaning rags and only toss away the section with a period stain. Your therapist has taught you to get in touch with your emotions and ask yourself, "Am I being rational or irrational?" You create an anonymous Yelp profile and give the therapist five stars and a blank review.

Be thirty, still trying to make a baby. If you don't get pregnant soon, you'll need to go for IVF with its plethora of needles. You thank God for your supportive husband and weekly therapy sessions as your period toys with you, bringing emotional pain and physical pleasure. One month your period doesn't come. You don't tell your husband. It's only three days late, and you're out of pregnancy tests. No point in running to the store when it's only been a couple of days. No need to get excited too early. Get in the shower, and your husband follows you in. He kisses you sweetly in the mischievous steam. Tell him shower sex will be difficult without the monthly lubrication. He looks at you funny and asks what you mean. Playfully paw at his chest and tell him your period is a little late. Watch for his reaction.

The words compute in his head, and then he looks at you wide-eyed and grinning. Smile at him tentatively and tell him you're going to get a test later today. "It's really too early to be hopeful." He hugs you under the warm, gushing water and whispers that he loves you either way. "Best case we have a baby," you whisper back. "Worst case, more period sex." Your heartbeat quickens, and as you feel the blood rush through your veins, you are full of vitality and joy.

CHAPTER TWELVE

WEEKEND RETREAT

"Thanks, Uncle Nick, we really appreciate you letting us borrow your cabin for the weekend," Candice heard her boyfriend Bobby say on the phone. Bobby had taken her, his best friend Carter, and Carter's girlfriend Zoe up to his Uncle's cabin to go hiking for a long weekend.

Bobby's uncle, a sixty-year-old bachelor, had built the cabin himself. The structure had two snug full-bed bedrooms, one bathroom with a clawfoot tub, and a surprising number of taxidermy animals. One particularly freaky fox, looking furiously happy, stood on a table in the main room while in the larger bedroom, a deer head hung above the dresser and always seemed to be looking at you no matter where you went in the room. Candice had asked to stay in the other smaller bedroom, which had a more sanguine taxidermy owl.

Be the perfect girlfriend for the next week and a half, and you should have a ring on your finger in three months, thought Candice leaning back on the plaid loveseat. Her mom had given her dad an ultimatum at the nine-month mark, and it had worked like a charm. While there were some road bumps, a tampon-sex incident, and Carter's general attitude toward her, in her gut, Candice knew she and Bobby were meant to be together. Bobby wanted the same things she did: a white picket fence, a pool in the backyard, and one to two children. Additionally, Bobby was kind, financially stable, and from a good family. He checked all of Candice's boxes.

Candice hadn't initially planned to push for an engagement in less than a year, but they made sense together. Sure, some of her friends thought Candice was being a bit rushed researching the perfect princess cut diamond, *but what's the point in waiting when you already know someone's the one?*

"God, doesn't the cabin smell great!" said Bobby once he hung up the phone. And it did smell pretty good, like pinecones and crushed leaves in the fall. "I can't believe Uncle Nick lent us this place."

"Definitely," said Candice, avoiding looking at the ecstatic fox. She'd worn black Athleta leggings and a houndstooth sweater for the drive up, her red hair in a stylized messy bun. "This place is positively perfect!"

"Look at that fox! Uncle Nick told me he shot it himself. Not that I'm a fan of shooting but look at it! So happy. You two match, the fur and the hair," said Bobby.

"Hope your uncle doesn't confuse me with a fox. I would hate to be shot," said Candice.

Bobby laughed fully, for a moment mirroring the fox's manic grin.

The heavy door to the cabin burst opened.

"We're back," said Carter loudly, coming through the entryway carrying a packed bag of groceries.

"We got everything on the list!" said Zoe with a smile, holding another two bags and following Carter in.

Though Carter and Zoe had been together for a few years, much longer than Bobby and Candice, the couples hadn't yet spent much time double dating. Because Carter had been

Bobby's best friend since Cub Scouts, Bobby had decided the long weekend was a great opportunity to ingratiate Candice with Carter and Zoe. Candice knew this was a sign of how serious Bobby was taking their relationship, but she wasn't enthusiastic about spending a weekend trapped with Carter. Since she'd agreed to the long weekend before she knew it would be an extended double date, Candice hadn't been able to coyly back out. Now, not only did Candice have to pretend to love the outdoors, but she also had to pretend to like sharing a one-bathroom cabin with someone she had the distinct impression did not like her.

Soon, they'd cooked dinner, eaten, and sat around by the fire, deciding where they'd go hiking the next day.

"Ooooh, look at Cloud Ridge," said Zoe, holding up her iPhone in its moss green Otter case. On the screen was a vista at sunrise looking onto rolling hills covered in the yellow, orange, and red leaves of fall.

"How many miles?" said Carter.

"Only 8.4," said Zoe.

"8.4 miles?" said Bobby, clicking his tongue. "Candice hasn't really been hiking before, so we'll want something shorter. Maybe five miles? Also, let's stick with moderate or easy. I don't want any of us falling off a cliff."

Candice shivered at the thought, and the fire crackled intensely.

"Makes sense," said Zoe, "I think my first hike was less than a mile." She laughed lightly, and Candice was thankful for the understanding in Zoe's tone.

"We won't be able to see much unless we hit a decent altitude," said Carter, leaning back, hands intertwined behind his head and elbows flared out like the fins of a space shuttle.

Turning to Candice, he cocked his head and asked, "Candice, you sure you can't handle a *real* hike?"

"Whatever you all agree on is good with me," said Candice with a smile when what she really meant was, *I know nothing about hiking, and you know that, prick.* "I'm going to go use the restroom." Candice didn't really have to pee, and she usually avoided going to the bathroom when other people could potentially hear her, but it was a good excuse to get away from Carter.

As she shut the door to the bathroom, she could hear Bobby saying, "Come on, Carter, be a team player."

Candice could feel the chill of the brown bathroom tiles through her socks. She peed and removed her tampon, wrapping it in the thin toilet paper. *Where's the bin?* thought Candice as she looked around the bathroom. There was no garbage, only the toilet, a plunger, and the clawfoot tub. The tampon had already begun soaking through its toilet paper wrapping, the smell mingling with the bathroom's pinecone scent. *Sorry Uncle Nick*, thought Candice as she dropped the tampon in the toilet and flushed. It swirled around the bowl lazily twice before heading downstream.

Candice removed a fresh tampon from the pocket of the leggings wrapped around her calves, looked at the plastic-covered tube for a second, and then put it back into the pocket. *Bobby's probably going to want to have sex tonight, and I don't want that to happen again.* Candice thought back to about two months ago when she and Bobby had accidentally had sex with her tampon still in. Candice hadn't even felt the tampon, but when she'd mentioned to Bobby finding it still inside her vagina, he'd gotten self-conscious that he had a small penis. After an hour, he put on an air of nonchalance, but Candice knew better. He'd even privately asked Carter about it, who'd commented Candice must have a stretched-out vagina. Candice had accidentally seen the concerned texts on Bobby's phone. After, she had reassured Bobby repeatedly that he had a normal-sized dick. Telling her boyfriend his penis was sufficient and having people talk about the size of her vagina was something Candice wanted to avoid in the future.

Glad I wore period panties, thought Candice as she washed her hands. Candice left the bathroom to find Bobby alone. Carter and Zoe had left.

"Let me guess, they went 'stargazing'?" said Candice playfully.

"Yup, also to have sex in the woods," said Bobby, smirking, a roguish glint in his eye.

"Clearly," said Candice. She pictured Carter and Zoe rolling around in the dirt. Candice wanted to be disgusted, but it sounded pretty hot if you forgot about ticks and mentally replaced Carter with her crush, Darren Barnet. Not that she, Candice, would ever forget about ticks.

"Should we move to the bedroom?" said Bobby suggestively.

"To stargaze?"

"Exactly," said Bobby.

Soon she and Bobby were making out, Candice on bottom, held between the rock-hard bed and Bobby's muscular body. Bobby started to make his way south, his head above her groin and his hands pulling at her leggings.

"Aunt Flo's mid-visit," said Candice.

"Huh," said Bobby as he tugged intrepidly at the constricting leggings.

"My period." Candice was breathing heavily, one hand knotted in her hair, the other gripping Bobby's shoulder.

"Oh," said Bobby and pulled away, "I'll get a towel. Actually, should we risk Uncle Nick's towels?"

"Whatever you want," said Candice, suddenly frozen awkwardly. Bobby paused to think through the situation, and as he did, Candice felt the gaze of the taxidermy owl watching her from atop an austere wooden dresser. She suddenly wished she'd chosen the room with the deer instead. Deer didn't have beaks and claws.

"Babe, how do you feel about doing it on the floor?" asked Bobby. "I know, not ideal, but it's easy to clean, plus you said you wanted to 'get in the outdoor spirit!'"

I'm going to get tetanus rolling around down there, thought Candice. What she said aloud was, "Umm, yeah, that sounds good, but can we check no nails are sticking out?"

Bobby eyed the floor, then threw his sweatshirt on the ground. "Problem solved!" he said assuredly.

Candice reluctantly got off the bed and gingerly sat on the ground atop the faded college sweatshirt.

Bobby sat next to her and leaned in for a kiss. After a minute, he pulled away and began to speak. "You know, I'm still okay with going down." His fingers danced across her thighs.

"We haven't done that before," said Candice, still distracted by the logistics of having sex on the studded wooden floor.

"I know," said Bobby.

"You don't think it's gross?" said Candice, muffling the unease in her own voice.

"No... I've actually done it before, and it didn't bother me."

No, you haven't, thought Candice. *Oh, he means with someone else*. Candice looked at Bobby, and his eyes glinted like a lion on the hunt. She suppressed a grimace.

"It can lead to really intense orgasms," said Bobby, still gently caressing her skin-tight leggings. "I think you'd really enjoy it, but only if you want me to."

Candice's head was dizzy. She and Bobby had been dating for over six months, but this was new. She pictured Bobby with a milk-stache made of menstrual blood. The thought made her gag.

"I think I'd rather stick to hand foreplay," said Candice. A glimmer of disappointment flashed in Bobby's face, but it was gone before Candice was sure it had been real or imagined.

"Your wish is my command," said Bobby and, as he kissed her again, she was enveloped by his scent, an overpowering men's deodorant.

Soon they were going at it like dogs, the floorboards creaking. Candice breathed heavily. Bobby grunted. The house moaned. In the distance, something gurgled, but Bobby and Candice thought of nothing but each other until he came on Candice's back.

"Sorry!" said Bobby. "It just happened so quickly. I think it's in your hair. Let me clean you up."

"Things happen," said Candice, shivering as she felt Bobby mop up her back with the underwear he'd previously been wearing. "I'm going to go rinse off." Candice grabbed her underwear off the floor, peeked out the bedroom door to ensure Carter and Zoe were still out and snuck to the bathroom still naked. Her knees hurt from the wooden floor, and her movements were spasmodic.

Candice scurried into the bathroom so quickly she hadn't noticed the puddle underneath her feet until the door closed behind her. While the toilet seat was down, it repeatedly flapped up, emitting bubbles of water like a filter in a goldfish bowl. The air in the room felt dank and smelled vaguely of a sewer.

"Bobby!" screamed Candice. "Bobby, I need your help!"

"Are you okay!" said Bobby, flinging open the door to the bathroom like a fireman in action. "Oh shit, the toilet!"

Bobby leaped around Candice, grabbing the plunger and flipping open the lid to the toilet, which flung bits of foul-smelling water in the air. Bobby thrust the plunger into the toilet, pushing even more fluid to waterfall over the rim and onto the tiled floor.

"Towels!" shouted Bobby.

Towels, where are the towels? Realizing she was literally standing next to what appeared to be a linen closet, she opened it to find an assortment of towels. Grabbing one, then another, she unfolded the towels and flung them on the floor until most of the surface area was covered. The towels quickly turned dark with water. Picking one up, she wrung it over the bathtub as Bobby continued to pump furiously.

"I think I got it!" said Bobby, reaching his hand into the toilet to pull something out.

The sound of the toilet flushing and loud laughter emanating from somewhere startled Candice, who turned around. Zoe and Carter stood at the doorway with Zoe wide-eyed and Carter laughing like a chimpanzee in the zoo. Candice kept turning, and she saw Bobby holding something in the air heroically. Something red and dripping. A bloody tampon. Her bloody tampon.

Candice felt the oxygen drain from her body. She had flooded the bathroom. Bobby was naked, smattered in period blood and toilet backwater with a semi-erect penis and holding her bloody tampon. She herself was naked, covered in the same disgusting mixture. Carter doubled over laughing.

Zoe hadn't moved. Candice's lungs felt as though they were imploding, and the bare skin all over her body felt like it was on fire.

Candice turned back, facing the tub. "Zoe, can you please close the door?" she managed to ask. After a moment, the door shut softly. "Bobby, I'm so sorry." The only sound in the room was the plinking of water droplets from the towel she'd been wringing over the tub.

"You flushed this?" said Bobby staring at the waterlogged tampon he held cupped in one hand.

"Do you want to put it down?" asked Candice.

"Where?"

Candice was silent.

"You know, this is my Uncle's place," said Bobby. "He built this cabin with his own two hands, and he honored me by letting us have this weekend. Why would you flush a tampon here? It's a septic system, for Christ's sake. Do you not respect him? Do you not respect me?"

"No, there's no garbage bin in here," said Candice hurriedly. "You were all sitting in the other room, and I didn't know what to do. It was a mistake."

"I understand mistakes, but you're not stupid."

"Yes, I am! I was stupid at the moment, and I'm so so sorry." The bathroom reeked of sewage.

Bobby rubbed his eyes with the hand not cupping the tampon. Candice worried the toilet water would give him pinkeye, but she stayed silent.

"Candice, please never again," said Bobby.

"Never," swore Candice.

"You're going to have to help me clean this up."

"Of course."

"God, Carter's going to give me shit for this. I hope he got poison oak up his ass tonight because at least that would distract him. I'm never going to hear the end of it."

"I know."

"I don't want him to blame you. Let's say it was, I don't know, a dead mouse that caused the blockage. Do you think Carter will buy that, or did he get too good a look?"

"He was too busy laughing," said Candice, her heart skipping a beat.

"Clean the floor up as best you can, and then let's hop in the shower. We can Clorox the room after," said Bobby. He stood confidently, wearing the splattered toilet water as if it was a badge of honor.

"There are no more towels," said Candice. "I mean, there are hand towels. The big ones are all on the floor."

"We'll make do tonight. I'm going to go throw this out. After we shower, we can throw the big towels in the tub and sanitize the floor."

"Bobby?"

"Yeah?"

"Thank you."

"Yeah, well, I love you," said Bobby, surveying the apocalyptic scene. After wrapping the tampon in fresh toilet paper, Bobby cupped his groin with his free hand. "Mind opening the door for me?"

Candice opened the door, and Bobby popped out to throw the tampon in the trash.

Candice turned on the shower and breathed a sigh of cautious relief.

First, he offers me period head because apparently that's a thing Bobby's into, and then I implode a toilet. At least he's not planning to tell Carter. No need to give that prick more ammunition. No matter what else happens, it's been a memorable weekend.

***

The next day they woke up bright and early for a hike. Bobby didn't mention the tampon and other than Carter making a crack about it being a nudist cabin, everyone seemed to have moved on. Once at the starting point for the hike, the boys scrambled ahead while Zoe took her time, allowing for Candice's beginner's pace. Candice could hear the wind whispering through the green trees. She and Zoe talked about the weather and work for a while until Zoe changed the subject.

"I know it was a tampon last night," said Zoe while waiting at the top of an incline Candice was struggling up.

Despite herself, Candice's face turned scarlet.

"Don't worry. Carter bought the whole mouse story. Too bad that toilet clogged." They were side by side now in a section of wide path laced with rocks and wooden branches. Zoe gracefully hopped over these hazards while Candice struggled not to trip.

"Can I ask you something?" said Candice, watching her feet navigate the rocky terrain.

"Yeah," said Zoe looking ahead.

"I really like Bobby, like I *really* like him. But he cares a lot about what Carter thinks, and clearly, Carter doesn't like me. I guess my question is, why doesn't Carter like me?" Candice was still breathing heavily and struggled through the words. Zoe, on the other hand, looked totally at home among the tall trees and spoke easily.

"I would lie and say Carter does like you, but that's not my style," said Zoe. She paused. "Carter says he doesn't think you're genuine. I told him no one's particularly honest in the first six months of a relationship, but I don't think that will change his opinion because I don't think that's the real reason he doesn't like you." Zoe casually pulled her hair into a low ponytail as she spoke. "I think Carter's threatened."

"Threatened?" said Candice. *Why would he be threatened by me?* She was so distracted by the idea she tripped on a branch, barely catching a tree trunk and preventing herself from falling to the ground.

"Be careful!" said Zoe. "Yeah, threatened. Carter's never really had to share Bobby before. Bobby's dated very few people for six months, and even then, he never seemed to like them as much as he clearly likes you."

Even the girls who didn't have massive vaginas, liked period head, and didn't implode toilets? "Huh," said Candice. "Any advice?"

"Hmm," said Zoe. "Ignore Carter. Don't get me wrong, I love my boyfriend, but he's as stubborn as a yak. Just because I was willing to wait years before truly breaking into the Carter-Bobby show doesn't mean you have to. Bobby likes you. I like you. Carter will come around."

"Thanks, Zoe. I'll have to think about that."

For a while, they hiked in silence, Candice busy with not tripping and processing this new information. *What does this mean for my nine-month plan? Are we on track, or am I rushing us because I'm secretly as insecure as Carter?*

"Oh my God, look," whispered Zoe. "A fox!"

Candice saw it, a small red fox about forty feet away. Unlike the freakily happy fox in the cabin, this one was calm and regal. It noticed them, almost nodding, and then turned to leave.

"Wow, I've never seen one on a hike before," said Zoe.

"Me neither. I mean, I've never been hiking before," said Candice. She breathed in deeply, her lungs expanding. The world felt bigger somehow, full of possibilities.

Zoe and Candice hiked for a while longer until they caught up with the boys at the summit. The view was breathtaking. Candice could see thousands of trees, clouds, and a lake so far away its surface looked as smooth as turquoise glass.

"Hope that wasn't too bad," said Bobby, pulling Candice close to him. His arm was strong, and his dried sweat smelled sweet. Candice kissed Bobby's cheek, marking him with her transparent Chapstick.

"You know, I didn't tell you, but I was worried about going on an outdoorsy trip and especially about hiking," said Candice admiring the horizon. "I'm really glad we did this. I'm enjoying the perspective."

"Yeah?" said Bobby. "I'm really glad to hear that. We can enjoy the view and then head back down for lunch. Don't want you getting famished and changing your mind about the joys of hiking." He gave her a squeeze.

"I'm in no rush," said Candice easily, her hair whisked back gently by the breeze. "Let's take our time and appreciate the journey."

CHAPTER THIRTEEN

NOT OKAY

Why did I think Target was the right place to buy a pregnancy test? Nancy thought. There had to be at least twenty different options on the shelf. Sticks that changed colors, sticks with plus signs, digital readers, one stick, two sticks, pink sticks, blue sticks. Too many options loomed in front of her.

Nancy's eyes, surrounded by large blotchy circles, jumped from box to box. Her full lips were red and raw from being chewed on, like rare hamburger meat. As she bit her bottom lip, she tasted metallic blood.

Just choose something, thought Nancy, but she couldn't choose. *If I don't choose soon, someone I know will see me here because I'm in a fucking Target. I should have gone to Walmart. No one luxuriously wanders the aisles in a Walmart, making eye contact and recognizing you. They go in, get what they need, and get out, making sure the entire time to avoid any potential human contact. That's what I should have done. Corwin would have known to go to Walmart.*

Nancy stood there paralyzed in a thought spiral, almost jumping out of her skin when another woman entered the aisle. Nancy stared at the woman who, without noticing

Nancy's transfixed gaze, grabbed a generic box of tampons and turned around to leave the aisle. Nancy felt her shoulders release, then immediately tense back up. *Oh shit, Jack's parents live around here. How can I explain the pregnancy test to them? "Oh, I'm not pregnant. This is for my roommate who moved out weeks ago." That wouldn't work. "Oh, I'm not pregnant. I'm just testing to see if I have cancer because I thought it might be contagious. Oh, that only works for testicular cancer? Oops."* Nancy jolted as if she'd been tasered by her thoughts. *What the fuck is wrong with me? Fuck. I wonder if his parents know about...* Nancy's thoughts trailed off, and her eyes began to water.

Jack and Nancy had been going out for about five months, and while things were good, she definitely wasn't ready to have his baby. Nancy wasn't ready to have anyone's baby, especially not with what was going on. She was still at the stage of life where "baby" referred to her boyfriend, not a literal infant. Anyway, she was confident Jack also wasn't ready to have a kid. He was a great boyfriend, but that didn't mean he was ready to change liquid diarrhea diapers in the middle of the night. Did it even matter, given the current situation? She hadn't told him about her missed period. Hopefully, she wouldn't have to, but she'd never missed a period before.

Nancy scanned the cultishly optimistic boxes again, finally plucking one and holding it in front of her smudged brown-frame glasses to examine the packaging. As she turned the box around to see the back, the remnants of a red manicure on her ragged fingernails glinted, making her hands resemble scratched claws. The fluorescent light above was almost too bright, and the text on the box glared at Nancy.

"Two tests for the price of one"… "six days sooner"… My period's already ten days late. This will do. Why do these bloody sticks cost so much?

Nancy placed the box in her cart, covertly nestling it next to the three-pack of lotioned tissues, and then covering it with the melting bags of frozen vegetables, brown rice, frozen dinners, Dove dark chocolate, and even more travel tissues. Once it was hidden, Nancy beelined through the towering aisles to self-checkout. Thankfully she had decided to purchase the pregnancy tests last.

***

In the car, with the three bags of groceries secured on the floorboard of the passenger seat, Nancy sat in the worn nylon driver's seat and closed her eyes. She clenched her shaking hands and breathed in for four seconds. With her hands still clenched, Nancy held her breath for another four seconds before letting go of it and her hands on a count of three. Nancy had learned this trick from Jack three weeks ago when the shit hit the fan. It was meant to slow her heart rate. Nancy repeated the pattern a couple of times before opening her eyes to the busy parking lot laden with abandoned carts and cars trying to park. She decided to focus on what was in front of her, another trick from Jack. Nancy could see the bumps in the faux leather steering wheel. She tried to memorize the texture while taking a few more breaths. Buying the pregnancy test had been the biggest distraction Nancy had had in the last three weeks, but it had only added to her stress.

Once her heart was no longer pumping the backbeat of "Bad Blood" by Taylor Swift, Nancy tore open the Dove bag and popped a chocolate in her mouth. She sucked on the melting chocolate and checked her phone. Jack had texted, "Love you, baby! See you as soon as I get back, and we can talk every night if you want. Keep breathing!" She put the phone down and decided she'd text Jack back later. There were no texts from Corwin. There hadn't been in weeks. Not even an irreverent meme.

Nancy's gradual meltdown had begun three weeks ago when Corwin, Nancy's roommate of the past four years and best friend, had been diagnosed with chronic lymphocytic leukemia. Nancy hadn't cried that first week, at least not in front of Corwin. Corwin had cried a lot. Corwin had cried, and packed, and cried some more. Corwin's father, Eric, an administrator at the Mayo Clinic in Rochester, Minnesota, had demanded Corwin come home immediately. Sadly Eric's mother, Corwin's grandmother, had died of cervical cancer the year before. Eric needed his only child home to take care of them. He couldn't lose anyone else. So a week after the diagnosis, Corwin was gone, and Nancy was left in the apartment to finish packing and shipping some of Corwin's boxes.

***

The bathroom was small and dank, the popcorn ceiling blotchy with water stains, and the lemon-colored paint bubbled with age. Nancy had always disliked sharing the apartment's single bathroom, especially one that smelled like an octogenarian's steam room, but over the last two weeks, she'd dreaded having it to herself. That morning Nancy had cried after noticing Corwin's missing lavender shampoo.

She knew Corwin was still very much alive, but Nancy wasn't sure how to process the loss of her roommate and friend and Corwin's future suffering. They used to spend hours every day talking, curled up on opposite ends of their worn periwinkle chenille loveseat. Once a week, they'd watched *The Bachelor* together, Nancy drinking Rosé and Corwin putting down a couple of Hefeweizen grapefruit beers. Whenever a show contestant's dress was particularly low-cut, Corwin would say "boobs" in a funny low-pitched voice, and Nancy would giggle. They'd talked about everything together, day-to-day bullshit to their hopes and dreams. One Sunday, Corwin had spent an hour describing the platonic ideal of bread to which Nancy had responded, "all bread is good bread," which simply led to Corwin spending another hour comparing the relative merits of sandwich bread, sourdough, and Corwin's favorite, bagels.

Since Corwin had left, they'd only talked once on the phone, and they hadn't talked about much at all. The phone call had been a nightmare, bizarre and unreal. Nancy, not knowing if or when she should call Corwin, had waited five days, longer than they'd gone without talking in years.

"Hi," Nancy had said tentatively. She'd sat on her side of the loveseat while staring at the eerie absence of Corwin. The armrest on Corwin's side still had a gash from when they, mid steampunk craze, had accidentally torn it with a bike chain bracelet. Corwin was always making grand movements, and Nancy had been relieved when Corwin retired that particular bracelet without further harm to their apartment.

"You still exist. I thought you'd moved on with your life," Corwin had said flatly.

"How are you doing?" Nancy had hazarded while picking at the fabric on her own armrest.

"I have *cancer*. That's a *stupid* question," Corwin had said bluntly, emphasizing the words cancer and stupid.

"Yeah," Nancy had responded, pausing in case Corwin wanted to say more. Silence had filled the line, and Nancy's mouth felt like it was full of cotton balls, dry and difficult to articulate. "How's your dad?"

"He cries more than I do," Corwin had said, and Nancy stifled a cooing noise into a small cough.

"Oh, that's rough," she'd said. Nancy had wished more than anything to hear Corwin's laughter. Corwin had a laugh that lit up a room, so jolly and full. But jokes were off-limits, potentially forever.

"Yeah," Corwin had said. The pauses were long and awkward.

"Do you want to hear about my week?"

"Sure," Corwin had said.

"Well, I've been staying at Jack's place, which you know is closer to my work, but he's going on a business trip in a week," Nancy had said, trying to sound normal. She was about to tell Corwin about how empty the apartment felt without them, how uncomfortably large this loveseat suddenly seemed, when Corwin cut her off.

"You know, I don't need your pity phone call." Corwin's voice had been sharp. "I get that you have this great life with a boyfriend and a job in the city, and I'm just some downer friend you lived with for a bit, but I'm dying, and I don't need you rubbing it all in my face." Something about Corwin's anger made them almost unrecognizable, like a familiar face under unfamiliar red light. Nancy felt her whole body in that moment. Her skin prickled as if being poked with thousands of needles.

"I didn't mean to..." Nancy had responded from the edge of her seat. She had been shaking so hard she thought she might tumble to the ground.

"Yeah, well, you did. I need to go. Don't bother calling again because I won't pick up." The line went dead.

Nancy, still shaking, had gripped her cellphone to her ear until her hand went numb. She'd stared the whole time at the gash in the loveseat.

Nancy hadn't called again. Corwin clearly needed some space, and she tried to respect that. Nancy had wanted to call or text every single day, but Corwin's words echoed in her head. *I don't need you rubbing it all in my face.* Jack told Nancy to give them some time, see if they reached out. Corwin was processing a lot of emotions. A week later, when Jack left town and Nancy realized her period was over a week late, she'd desperately wanted to call Corwin for advice and consolation. She'd stopped herself. *How can I call Corwin about a pregnancy scare when Corwin is dealing with the big C? How can I make this about me right now?*

***

Settling down on the chilly porcelain toilet, Nancy carefully read and reread the package. Thankfully for Nancy's scrambled brain, it was simple: pee on the stick mid-stream and then wait two minutes. Extracting one of the two plastic pouches, Nancy opened it and took the cover off the stick. She delicately held the protruding strip where she hoped the pee would come out. Nancy knew pee came out of the urethra, which was sandwiched between the clitoris and the vaginal canal, but with her head in a haze, that information was useless.

Nancy peed a little, missing the stick before course correcting. Once she managed to get a couple of seconds of pee on the stick, she stopped and stared at the device as the fluid traveled through the papery material. First, one line appeared, then a second formed in parallel. No third line, which would have formed a plus sign, appeared. Nancy placed the cover back over the bit she'd peed on and then put it flat on the minuscule linoleum counter next to her. She set her phone's alarm for two minutes. She tried closing her eyes and breathing, but her heartbeat was too fast and distracting. Opening her eyes, she stared at the pregnancy test. It hadn't changed. Furtively looking between the countdown on her phone and the stick, the seconds slowly ticked by along with her shallow breaths. The alarm went off gleefully. Nancy wasn't pregnant, probably.

Nancy then took the second pouch from the box, quickly tearing open the plastic and whipping off the cap. She peed again, this time carefully waiting till mid-stream to place the stick under her flow. Replacing the cap on this stick, she placed it tactfully next to its twin on the blotchy bathroom counter. This time she set the alarm and didn't look.

Instead, Nancy stared at the single piece of art in the bathroom, Corwin's poster of *The Great Wave off Kanagawa* from the Thirty-Six Views of Mount Fuji collection. When they'd moved out, they'd said Nancy should toss the poster, that they knew Nancy didn't like it, and they didn't care if she kept it. But Nancy hadn't tossed the poster. It was Corwin's poster, and Corwin belonged in their apartment.

Before the diagnosis, Corwin had loved the wave, always talking about how the artist had magically captured the movement of water with woodblocks. Until this moment, waiting for the pregnancy test results, Nancy had never felt the movement or understood Corwin's love of the piece. Now the wave seemed to be rushing at her. After two minutes, the phone began blaring a cloying ringtone, jarring Nancy from her thoughts of the water. After turning it off, she peaked cautiously at the stick. Then, there it was, two lines in parallel. No plus sign. She wasn't pregnant.

Thank Jesus.

Nancy dry heaved. Her fingertips prickled, and her head felt like a balloon drifting off among fluffy clouds in a sunny sky. She sat there, soaking in this physical wash of relief. After a few minutes and more than a couple of re-checks of the pregnancy tests, her body began to return to her. But there was one thought that wouldn't go away and made her spine tingle: *If I'm not pregnant, why don't I have my period?*

Nancy went back on her phone and frantically searched, "Why is my period missing?" Quickly she ruled out the first reasons she scrolled across.

No weight gain or loss and no excessive exercise. I can't even remember the last time I went to the gym... I really should go to the gym. Maybe it'll help with the crying.

Nancy kept scrolling.

Stress can cause late periods?

Nancy considered this possibility. In the past, stress had never affected her periods. Not even taking her first architect's licensing exam, the most stressful test of her life, had influenced her cycle. Instead, Nancy had cramped terribly the day of the exam and bled through her pants.

Nancy kept reading the online article. No, she was definitely not perimenopausal or on a new medication, and though apparently changing time zones could throw off a cycle, the only instance she'd changed time zones in the last year was for Daylight Savings.

It must be stress. I'm not pregnant, so it must be stress. The stress of possibly being pregnant? No, that would only make

*sense if I was in a Christopher Nolan movie... Corwin. I'm
an idiot.*

Nancy got up, washed her numb hands with icy water,
then began to pace her apartment, feverishly turning back
and forth in the small common room. Suddenly she stopped
in place, pulled out her phone, and began going through
her recent contacts. There was Jack, her mom, a friend
named Antonia. Finally, Nancy found who she wanted and
clicked call. The tone rang three times, and then a dull voice
picked up.

"Hello?"

"Corwin! Don't hang up! I need to say thank you." She
was too happy and sad at the same time not to tell Corwin.
This has gone on too long.

"Oh God, Nancy, if you thank me for the impact I've had
in your life, I will vomit. I will literally vomit and hang up.
My Uncle Clark tried that on me yesterday," lamented Corwin. Corwin sounded frustrated but not as angry as the last
time they'd spoken. Nancy bounced on the balls of her feet,
ecstatic at the sound of Corwin's voice.

"You know how much we hate our periods, right?" asked
Nancy as she continued to pace back and forth across
the living room. It was only a dozen steps across, so she
turned frequently.

"Yes," said Corwin with tender caution.

"I wanted to thank you for literally stressing my period
away and also wanted to let you know we're probably no
longer in period sync. I'm sorry about that. Now that you've
gifted me a month without cramping and saved me at least
six dollars on tampons, five pounds of water weight, and
hours of watching shitty rom-coms, I'll be using the savings and some discretionary cash to ship you bagels from

Pammies. It's heartbreaking that there are no good bagel places in Minnesota."

Nancy continued quickly, worried that Corwin might hang up. "Further, from now on, I'll be calling every day at 9 p.m. in case you want to talk. I can't promise I'll say the right things. I probably won't, but I'll always be here. If you don't pick up when I call the first time, I'll call another two times to break through the do-not-disturb setting you annoyingly always have on. If you still don't pick up, I promise I won't leave voicemails because I know how much you hate them. Also, though we haven't been texting recently, going forward, you should expect at least one cute baby animal or meme a day. You're my best friend, not just a roommate I lived with for a while. I *refuse* to let you go." Nancy paused to take some deep breaths and to wait for Corwin's response. She wasn't sure if it would work. The vague trembling in Nancy's hands had grown to a strong quake. The line was quiet while the radiator in the corner of the room clanged angrily.

"Nancy..." said Corwin, their crackling voice breaking the silence. "You abandoned me... I got sick, and you weren't there."

"I know," said Nancy, her own voice breaking, "I was trying to give you space, and that was a mistake. The biggest mistake. Corwin, please, *please* give me another chance."

"I don't know what to say," said Corwin.

"Say that I can visit you next month for my vacation."

"Maybe," said Corwin, and Nancy could hear them sniffling. "But absolutely no pity."

Nancy stopped pacing. "No pity, I promise."

"Fine," said Corwin. "You can visit. It's been weird not seeing you every day since I moved back here."

"It's been weird not having you home," said Nancy, gingerly settling into her side of the loveseat. "Your room's waiting for you if you want to move back in. I even kept your poster in the bathroom." She rubbed the gentle chenille with her left hand, and its broken-down smoothness calmed her.

"I wish," responded Corwin. "Nope, you'll have to survive on your own."

"We both know I make stupid decisions when I'm on my own. Because you weren't here, I made the ignoramus move of going to Target on Main Street to buy a pregnancy test."

"Don't Jack's parents live right by that Target?" said Corwin, the fullness returning to their voice.

"Exactly!" said Nancy, sinking into the couch, her head leaning comfortably against the backrest.

"That is dumb. Why didn't you go to Walmart? Cheaper, and no one would recognize you," said Corwin.

"Because I'm an idiot without you."

"Wait, did you tell Jack about the pregnancy test?" asked Corwin.

They continued talking for the next hour, covering everything from Nancy's pregnancy scare, to Corwin's chemo, to what bagel flavors Nancy should send and the merits of poppy seeds.

"I'll see you in person soon, and in the meantime, virtual watch part of *The Bachelor* tomorrow?" said Nancy as the conversation was winding down.

"Obviously, though, I'm not really supposed to drink," said Corwin.

"Get one of those fancy fruit juices you like," said Nancy, picturing the bright orange and green drinks Corwin used to have stocked in their fridge. "I'll have a lemonade."

"Sounds good. I have to run, but before I go, um… Nancy, you should know you're my best friend and that I love you."

In sickness and in health, thought Nancy.

"Corwin, I love you too. Goodbye, at least until tomorrow at 9 p.m. eastern."

"Bye," said Corwin and hung up.

Nancy grabbed her car keys from the end table and headed to Target to buy some lemonade with her shoulders back, and head held high.

I should buy some Chapstick while I'm there. Target has that organic brand I like, or maybe I'll try something new; they have so many options. Ha, I guess I'll take my time deciding while I luxuriously wander the aisles. I'll have to text Corwin for their opinion. Asking Corwin is always the right choice.

CHAPTER FOURTEEN

BLOODY HELL

I insert a manicured finger into my vagina and feel for the cup. Maneuvering the finger up from the popsicle stick bit, I reach for the cup's plastic edge and run around the rim in a circular motion to ensure the cup is fully sealed. It is.

This is the first time I'm touching myself this intimately in years. Not that I don't masturbate. I actually masturbate weekly as part of my wellness routine (aimed at freeing my mind of distractions so I can focus my energy on my goals), but when I masturbate, I use the correct tools. Why finger myself like a cavewoman when I can achieve orgasm more quickly with precision technology? I highly recommend the Lily Allen Liberty by Womanizer to all my female connections when the subject comes up. Speaking of technology, I know the menstrual cup isn't anything new, but it is new to me. It's a new year, and it's time for a new menstrual product.

As a big fan of New Year's Resolutions, I've had my fair share. Three years ago, I committed to getting a job as a paralegal. Crushed it. Two years ago, I committed to acing the LSAT. Crushed it again. And last year, I committed to applying to law school. While I haven't heard back yet, I am confident I'm going to continue on my streak of absofuckinglutely crushing it. What can I say? I'm fabulous, hardworking, and beautiful. A true triple threat.

Earlier this year, to distract myself from pending law school admissions decisions, I resolved to live a greener life, starting with my period products. My argument for this resolution was both the eco ramifications and financial. Why should I spend $6 a month ruining the planet with tampons and their plastic applicators when, for $30, I can get a menstrual cup that lasts ten years? I'm not excited about having to insert, remove, and regularly clean a cup, but as someone who's about to accrue a lot of student debt, it's a good time to be frugal. A verdict is reached, and the court decides in favor of the cup!

Today is the day. After months of research, it is finally time to give this cup a run for my money. And honestly, since insertion, today is going great.

Despite the bumpy bus ride, I make it to the office with barely a hair out of place. In the bathroom, I confirm that my panty liner is as clean as fresh snow. Next, I crush all of my morning papers. All my work consists of reviewing millions of papers, checking my email, and then reviewing more papers. It's a Sisyphean task about as pleasant as simultaneously stabbing both my eyes with dull forks, but it's going to get me into law school, so it's worth it. When I applied for the job, I thought working at a law firm would be exciting, even as a lowly paralegal, but looking back at the last two years it's been a very boring beige. The office always smells like burnt coffee, and every day it's one page after the next. Therefore, I constantly remind myself that this job is worth it for two reasons. First, it's getting me into law school. Second, it's got good health benefits.

Looking at the clock, it's almost eleven. Time to empty my cup! I remove the travel bottle of antimicrobial soap I'd prepared in my bag and hide it up my sleeve, just like I've done with a tampon every previous month. As one of three women in a twenty-person office, I've heard many of the more senior men joke about the time of the month their wives go *crazy*. No one in this office is ever going to know when it's my "crazy" time of the month.

"Lunch in five?" I say to Daryl and Raj, two of the three other paralegals. Sebastian, the fourth paralegal, is out on vacation. It's been nice not having to deal with Sebastian. As the most tenured paralegal at the firm, he's cocky. Plus, he's still butt hurt that I wouldn't go on a date with him. He doesn't explicitly mention it anymore since that might give me grounds to file a complaint with HR (Tanya, one of the two other women in the office) and get him reprimanded, but I can hear it in the way he talks to me. I'm sorry, but I expect men to respect my choices, and I choose not to shit where I eat. I've thought it through, and if I'm going to break my rule about not dating colleagues, it certainly won't be for you, Sebastian. Maybe I'd entertain the advances of a senior partner, but the current partners are all too old, ugly, and married. Until someone worthy of me makes partner, my office rule is they can look, but they can't touch.

"Sure," says Daryl, barely glancing up from a stack of papers thicker than an encyclopedia.

"Mmm," grunts Raj in agreement, not even looking up.

I walk across the office to the bathroom. The office was originally a condo building built in the seventies and, during the conversion, they'd left the beige carpeting in the bathroom. If it didn't reek of disinfectant, I might think I was in my great Aunt's house. There's even a bath-shower combo with a matching beige curtain.

Locking the door, I slide the bottle of antimicrobial soap out of my sleeve and onto the counter while I check my hair in the mirror. It needs a minor smoothing but is otherwise flawless.

Replace the cup or pee first? Argument for the cup: Replacing the cup first is probably more sanitary. Argument against: If I pee first, there will be less pressure making the cup easier to remove. Further, the argument for replacing the cup first is logically flawed. Because I'll be washing the cup with the antimicrobial soap, the order makes no difference for hygiene purposes. Argument against wins. I'll pee first.

When going to the bathroom, I usually fully take off my skirt and hold it on one arm while using the other to pee. This accomplishes two objectives, keeping the skirt off of the ground and reducing the likelihood of wrinkles. Today I need both my arms free. So, after checking that the counter is clean, I take my skirt off, fold it, and place it next to the sink. Next, I do the same with my underwear. I also remove two sparkling fashion rings. Once this is all settled, I pee and pat myself thoroughly dry. Now it's time to remove the cup.

Inserting my pointer finger into my vagina, I sail past the cup's stem to the base. This had been the tricky part during my practice run last week, but I know what I'm doing this time. I press the finger into the base in order to break the seal, then grasp both sides of the cup's stem and rock it gently back and forth while pulling down. Then things suddenly go terribly, disastrously wrong.

With a squelching sound reminiscent of a bad porno movie, the cup comes out. What I hadn't counted on was what would happen when the cup unfurled after it exited the physical constraints of my vagina. Yes, I had read I should continue to pinch the base as I removed the cup, but I am so focused on pulling the stem I forget to pinch. As soon as the cup leaves my vagina, it pops into its unconstrained bell shape, and this expansion bursts blood and small clumps up and out. I feel the blood hit my stomach and watch it smatter the bottom of the shower curtain and a large patch of the floor. It isn't a lot of blood, but it is the dark red of dying roses and now speckles everything around me. The whole space suddenly smells like a woman's locker room.

I was supposed to pinch it. Everything would have been fine if I'd just pinched. Instead, I am in a Jackson Pollock themed horror movie. I rub my chin only to feel thick blood smear against my skin.

Why didn't I pinch? Oh my God, I was supposed to pinch it. Oh my God, they are going to fire me. This is property damage. They're going to sue me. I'm not going to get into law school. They're going to revoke my recommendation. I'm going to be barred from the law. I'm going to have to move to Canada. Why didn't I pinch? I knew I was supposed to pinch!

Think, Aoife, *think*. Can I sue them? No, wait, what are my options, my arguments.

Leave the scene of the crime, pretend it wasn't me. Arguments for: I can get away with it. Men know nothing about periods and wouldn't suspect me. They'd think someone went psycho and tried to murder a squirrel in here. Arguments against: No one's going to believe in squirrel murder. This place smells like heat, and men aren't that stupid. Well, maybe the junior lawyers are that stupid, but what about the partners and the other women! Someone's going to realize this is period blood, and there are only three women in this office, and the other two sure look postmenopausal. Okay, leaving the scene is not an option.

Next case, ask for help. Arguments for: I need help. Arguments against: I could lose my job, my recommendation, and law school. I could lose law school. I can't lose law school. No, next option. Remove the evidence. Arguments for: Without evidence, the case can't go anywhere. People flush drugs all the time and get away with it. I can flush the cup, and it would be like this never happened. Plus, if it floods the bathroom, they might think the blood was part of the toilet backup. Arguments against: If they do figure it out, property damage liability could put me in permanent debt. Let's keep this one on the table as Remove the Evidence subpoint a.

Option Remove the Evidence subpoint b—cleanup but don't flush the menstrual cup. Arguments for: I saved my favorite white cashmere sweater after that ice skating incident, so if I can get the blood out of the carpet, maybe no one will ever have to know. Arguments against: I don't have access to OxyClean, so this plan depends on soap, water, and maybe some salt working. Yes, salt and cold water. That works on blood. There's salt in the breakroom. I think this is my strongest case.

I am rocking back and forth on the toilet, and I stop myself to analyze the blood. It had begun to set and dry on the shower curtain and carpet. I realize I am still holding the cup by its stick and immediately pour the remaining contents, a heterogeneous mix of thick blood and clumps, in the toilet. It's disgusting. Why did I ever get involved with a menstrual cup? Never mind that now, I don't have time for the regret that is creeping in. I get up and begin scrubbing the menstrual cup in the sink with my special-purpose soap. Glancing up in the mirror, I look terrible.

There's blood on my face, and my hair, and my *silk shirt!* What was I thinking? Okay, what was I thinking? Positives, I'm saving the world one period at a time, it's not on my skirt, and the bit on my shirt can be tucked in. This will be okay. I only need to reinsert the cup, clean my face and hair, and get the salt. Oh wait, should I try soap and water first or salt? I know cold water and salt works, but that means leaving the bathroom, and someone else could come in and see this war zone. That's not an option. Okay, cold water and soap it is.

I take off my top, turn on the cold tap, and delicately put the spots with blood under the running water. Quickly, most of the shirt is drenched. I lay it flat on the opposite side of the sink from the folded skirt and blot the blood spots with toilet paper. The toilet paper is soon covered in pale pink circles. I'm not sure how long I continue blotting, but next, I wipe down the wall and begin working on the carpet on my hands and knees.

A knock at the door startles me. "Aoife, it's Raj. Daryl wants to go to lunch." The door is thin, and the voice is clear, almost as if Raj is in the bathroom with me.

Oh my God, I'm naked. I'm crawling on the flooring wearing only my black lace bra. All of my clothes, *including my underwear,* are on the counter. Hell, I'm not even wearing my stilettos; they're sitting by the toilet. I'm naked at work! Did I lock the door?

"Hi Raj," I can hear myself saying. "You and Daryl should go to lunch without me." This isn't really happening. None of this is real.

"Are you sure? You've been gone for a while. Are you okay?" says Raj through the door. Stupid try-hard Raj, he only joined the firm a couple of months ago straight out of school, and now he's questioning me? I mean, I guess I shouldn't judge him for being a try-hard because I'm a try-hard… but no newbie should be questioning me. I've been at this firm for almost three years.

"I'm fine, please go," I strain.

"Do you want Daryl and I to bring you back any lunch, or medicine, or anything?" asked Raj. His voice irritates me. *You're not a good person, Raj. You're a try-hard.*

"No," I say.

"Well, if you change your mind, text me! We'll be back soon, and I can be back sooner if you need anything," says Raj.

"Thank you," I say.

"Bye Aoife, be back soon."

"Bye," I say.

I hear Raj's footsteps walk away from the door. I am still frozen, hunched over next to the toilet with my bare spine arched, like a sorority girl about to barf next to the toilet because she's too drunk to puke into the bowl. Not my fondest memories. Even so, I was always at my morning classes five minutes before they began.

I am back to dabbing the ground furiously with a wet tissue. The office has plush toilet paper, which I'm generally thankful for (sometimes I even sneak a roll in my bag when I'm running low at home), but for cleaning up blood it's a nightmare. It's not holding together. Instead, it keeps turning into balls of fluff as I rub.

After twenty minutes on the floor and another ten minutes on the shower curtain, I examine my efforts. The carpet's flecks are now faint. Still there, but faint enough that they could be mistaken for age spots. The shower curtain is worse, clearly showing a line of splatter marks. I need salt. Time to get dressed, but first the cup. This cup is going to kill me. Or kill my chances at getting into law school, which would basically be the same thing. I reinsert the cup with surprising ease, then put back on my underwear, wet shirt, and skirt. I sneak out of the bathroom like it's a one-night stand, shutting the door behind me. Thankfully the office is empty for lunch, and I am able to patter to the kitchen, grab the salt, and get back to the bathroom without seeing a soul.

I pour little piles of salt on the flecks on the carpet, rubbing them in with my thumb. Next, I take the shower curtain down and pour salt on its spots as well. It proves harder to clean, so I fold up the fabric to bring home. Since I work with men, they're pretty oblivious and shouldn't notice the missing curtain. Even if they do, they'll probably think the cleaning staff took it. That's not an extraordinary guess.

I drop water on the salt spots, and they dissolve into the rug. They're clearly wet but otherwise unremarkable. Looking around, I'm pretty satisfied. Besides the missing shower curtain, the bathroom looks as bland and condo-like as normal. I'm done. With this relief, I feel it. Ah shit, I need to poop. Usually, I only poop at home, but the adrenaline of the last forty minutes has affected my digestive system. At least the office is probably still empty.

I sit down on the toilet, placing some of the remaining toilet paper in the bowl to prevent skid marks. Before bearing down, I insert one finger into my vagina to hold the menstrual cup in place.

At least I prepared for this and remember what to expect. After reading horror stories online of women going to the bathroom and accidentally birthing their menstrual cups into automatically flushing toilets, the instructions of how to poop with a menstrual cup in are emblazoned in my brain. As I bear down, I feel the cup moving and pressing against my finger. It really does want to pop out again, but I won't let it.

Not till I get home. I will not be defeated by a menstrual cup. I will beat this thing. I finish pooping, the cup still in place.

I did it. I am a capable person. I can use a menstrual cup, and maybe I will go to law school.

I flush the toilet and my doubts, wash my hands again, and then leave the bathroom. I shove the shower curtain in my bag before anyone comes back from lunch. Grabbing a spare cardigan and a Luna bar from my desk drawer, I button the cardigan over my damp shirt and then eat the bar. It is dry and unappetizing. When Raj and Daryl come back from lunch, I am already working. When they ask about me, I mention bad breakfast food and gesture to my stomach before shuffling some papers. This detail is embarrassing enough for them to nod and change the subject. We all get back to work. I am moist and unfocused, but over the next four hours, I dry off and get some work done. The office buzzes with its regular noises, doors opening and shutting, coffee brewing, the AC humming. Thankfully, no one mentions the wet bathroom carpet for the rest of the day.

The next day I return the shower curtain. After some OxyClean, it's pristine. No one has noticed the almost imperceptible stains on the carpet. I am still wearing my menstrual cup, but today I cleaned it at 7 a.m., so I won't have to empty it again until after work. I vow to never empty my menstrual cup at work again. This is a small sacrifice for winning the war. I have beaten the menstrual cup. I am victorious. That night, I get my first law school acceptance. Then, I empty my cup without issue.

CHAPTER FIFTEEN

ALL TOO WELL

—

As if this week wasn't bad enough, Hunter began to gush blood out of her vagina.

Fuck this, Hunter thought as she removed the plastic backing of the monstrous maxi pad and attached it to her underwear. As she sat on the toilet, blood continued to leak out of her like the apartment's broken kitchen faucet. Drip, drip, drip. She'd told the landlord about the kitchen sink weeks ago, but the oily man hadn't done a thing about it.

Twenty-nine and there she was, in her 300-square-foot West Village studio apartment, masturbating to try and relieve her period cramps. Her libido wasn't working, so after five minutes she gave up. Hunter grabbed some toilet paper and began to try and clean up the mess.

God, I need a wax. What do I have to be thankful for? Fucking nothing. Fuck Thanksgiving. Fuck America. Fuck Charlie. Hunter began to tear up.

Having grown up in Canada with parents who hated each other, Hunter had been really excited about Thanksgiving in America. A new holiday for her to celebrate, unblemished by her past. After she'd moved countries, it hadn't been what she expected. She'd been in America for the past four years and, for three of those Thanksgivings, she'd been alone. It was almost as if Hunter was doomed to unhappy holidays until this year. This year was supposed to be the year she had a real American Thanksgiving. She was supposed to be with Charlie. She was supposed to be in Vermont, eating turkey and spiked hot cocoa. She was supposed to be anywhere but in this suffocating apartment.

Hunter pulled up her matted fuzzy pajama bottoms and flushed the toilet. Rinsing her hands without soap—she'd run out on Monday—Hunter then slinked out of the bathroom to the only other room in her apartment.

Probably should have used some shampoo on my hands. Fuck it, thought Hunter. *Stupid 'silk shampoo' probably would have made them smell worse. Not that it makes a difference to me.* Hunter was anosmic, meaning she lacked a sense of smell. Like many chronic anosmics, as a child, Hunter had repeated sinus infections that killed her olfactory cells. Those cells never grew back.

Opening the freezer, Hunter grabbed the strawberry ice cream bucket, then a spoon from the mostly empty drawer, and got into bed. The room was a war zone. The laundry bucket was overflowing, though Hunter didn't know how that was possible. She'd been in the same pair of pajamas for the past three days. *I probably smell, but people alone on Thanksgiving* are *allowed to smell bad*, she justified to herself.

The sink contained every IKEA bowl she owned, six of them, with remnants of cereal and chunky milk as well as an assortment of used plates and cups. A large ice cream stain stared back at her from the gray rug, and all of her small couch's cushions lay scattered on the remaining floor space. She'd thrown them there after telling Charlie she didn't want to go to his Thanksgiving anyway.

The change of direction in their relationship was enough to give Hunter whiplash. Six months ago they'd met through an app, and until the breakup Hunter thought it was going to be her fairytale.

After finishing residency, Charlie had recently moved to Manhattan, where they'd gone on their first date in a Tribeca bar.

"So, what kind of doctor are you?" Hunter had asked in the lowlights of the bar.

"Gynecologist," said Charlie, looking into Hunter's hazel speckled eyes as if challenging her to react. Hunter held steady. At least he was cute and a doctor, albeit a gyno.

"Hm."

"Does it bother you? It bothers some women."

"Not me," Hunter lied, quickly taking a sip of her red wine. "How'd you get into that?"

"Short answer, four older sisters. One bathroom." Charlie smiled. It was a crooked smile with dimples.

Hunter laughed. "Four older sisters, and you still wanted to be around women all day? Good for you." Hunter playfully twirled a piece of her long cocoa-colored hair. Subtle jazz music hummed from behind the bar. "Tell me a gynecologist fact."

"Uhhh, what's one that won't scare you off…"

"I don't scare easily."

"Well, labiaplasty, cosmetic surgery of the vagina, is on the rise. A lot of women seem to think their inner labia should be small, like when they were children, but it's actually normal for a woman to have inner labia that protrude past the outer labia or are asymmetrical. Surgery is an unnecessary medical risk and a waste of money if you ask me." He paused and sipped his drink, something brown and murky, while looking at her over the glass. *He's testing me,* Hunter had thought. "But enough about my job, what do you do?"

The conversation quickly moved on from gynecology to office politics as Hunter and Charlie sipped and chatted about her job in telemarketing. The night faded into smiles, giggles, and their two faces very close together. They'd even accidentally bumped noses.

Now, six months later, Charlie hadn't exactly uninvited Hunter to Thanksgiving, but what he had done was somehow almost worse.

"I'm not sure I can be with someone who doesn't take care of themselves." What the fuck does that mean? Prick, thought Hunter as she shifted her heating pad onto her midriff, then opened the ice cream carton to find it was empty. *Oh fuck, I put it in the freezer so I wouldn't have to take out the trash.* Next to the door, her pink baby-sized trash can was overflowing, and a crushed tissue box and an empty bag of Fritos lay next to it on the ground.

I mean, obviously, right now, this place is a mess, but this is Charlie's fault. We may or may not be in the middle of a breakup. Why didn't I see this coming?

The first three months of Hunter and Charlie had been blissful. She'd never dated anyone who actually owned a picnic basket, let alone take her on a picnic in the botanical gardens for a third date. They had their first kiss there. It was gentle, and he'd tasted like sweet honey. Hunter had never wanted it to end.

Soon after, they spent every weekend and some weeknights together at his place when he wasn't on call. He'd visited hers a handful of times, commenting how "cute" it was. He was right. It was cute. For his first visit, she'd washed her comforter (possibly for the first time ever; she wasn't sure), purchased the baby-sized pink trash can (a friend had remarked that her old trashcan smelled), and actually hung the framed family photo her mom had sent her after Christmas. It was the one they'd taken last year at her new step-dad Jerry's house. Hunter didn't like Jerry and suspected Jerry didn't like her, but at least they looked like a happy family.

Honestly, Hunter couldn't pinpoint when the crack first appeared between her and Charlie, but it might have been their first trip together four months in. Hunter wasn't great about tracking her period, so it came as a surprise when she started cramping on the long drive to Montauk. Charlie was at the wheel when Hunter let out an unconscious groan.

"You okay?" Charlie had said with his brow knitted as he looked away from the road to Hunter.

Hunter had sat up straight in her seat, her head almost butting the car's ceiling. "Oh no!" she exclaimed.

"What is it, sugar?" said Charlie. The car's AC could barely keep up with the surprising September heat, and the light beat down on them through the windows.

"Charlie, I am so sorry. I'm getting my period. I thought it was coming later this week or next weekend." Despite their four blissful months together and Charlie being a gynecologist, Hunter had been avoiding period talk for fear it would impact the honeymoon phase. After that first date with Charlie, he hadn't talked about his work much except to mention office politics, and Hunter didn't want to bring vaginas into their relationship. She'd manage to move or cancel plans with him the last couple of times she'd been menstruating. Thankfully her period really only lasted two and a half days, though the first twenty-four hours were always rough.

"Oh, that's fine. You don't need to apologize! What does your period mean for you, and how can I support you on this trip?" asked Charlie. Charlie and Hunter were on their way to Charlie's friend John's Montauk home for the weekend. Hunter had only met John and his fiancée Mackenzie a couple of times, and she was really excited to make a good impression while also enjoying the last of summer weather.

Hunter bit her lip, then remembered she was wearing lipstick and quickly unbit.

"Do you mind if we stop somewhere for me to get some products?

"Of course, I mean of course not. We'll stop at the next service station. If you want, I have some ibuprofen in the glove box."

"Oh, no thanks. I don't take medication unless it gets really bad. You know, not too many drugs if I can stand it," said Hunter casually. The car sped up, getting a little closer to the black Toyota that had been in front of them for the last hour. Charlie was a middle lane driver, and when that wasn't an option, a right lane driver. He rarely got closer than fifty feet to the car in front of him.

"Hm, does it get bad often? I hate to have you in pain," said Charlie.

The hairs on Hunter's arm tickled, and she scratched them.

"About half the time," said Hunter. For a moment, there was only the humming of the road and the glaring sun.

"You know, you really shouldn't be concerned about taking ibuprofen for cramps. If you're going to take an NSAID, it's better to take it sooner because they only prevent future pain. The drugs don't reduce pain you already have."

Hunter had awkwardly said she didn't want the drugs, and Charlie had said he was supportive of whatever she wanted. But Hunter didn't feel supported. Later that night, when she had asked for the ibuprofen, she'd felt judged by his puppy dog eyes. Things had been good enough with John and Mackenzie, but she and Charlie both knew she wasn't as talkative as normal, and it made her feel guilty. Then, that night when it was time for bed, things had gotten even worse.

Normally, Charlie held her at night, but instead, he'd asked for some space. He was so far to one side of the bed Hunter thought he'd fall off. When she tried to ask him about it, he mentioned having a headache, but that certainly didn't explain why he didn't so much as kiss her goodnight. Was it because she hadn't talked enough with Mackenzie?

When Hunter had woken up in the night, Charlie wasn't even in the bed. It was still dark outside, and in the shadows, Hunter had thought Charlie must have really fallen off, but he wasn't on the ground, and his side of the bed was neat. She had tiptoed through the creaky house in her brand-new nightdress to find Charlie asleep on a couch. She'd poked him. His head had bobbed, but he was still asleep.

She had pushed his shoulder harder and whispered, "Charlie!"

Charlie had woken.

"Hunter... uh Hunter, what time is it?" Charlie had said groggily.

"Not even 5:30," said Hunter, staring down at him. His face had a slight floral-shaped indent from the cushions. *How on Earth did he sleep on that? Why did he sleep on that?* thought Hunter at the time.

"Okay," said Charlie, and he had barely lifted his head, "you gonna shower?" The house had creaked eerily in the darkness.

"No, Charlie, it's not even 5:30," Hunter had said. "You coming back to bed? I have an alarm set for seven, and I was planning to shower then."

"Good, shower," Charlie had gurgled. Hunter had waited, but Charlie's eyes stayed closed.

"Is something wrong, Charlie? I want to go back to sleep." Hunter had shivered in her delicate nightgown.

"No, go," Charlie had said, only his hand moving on the sofa, gesturing her to leave. Hunter had stood over him, her toes fiddling on the ground.

"Are you coming?" Hunter had said.

"No," Charlie had said into the fabric.

"Can I ask why not?"

"Smell."

"Smell?"

"Sorry, no, it's stuffy in the room," Charlie had said, opening his eyes.

Hunter had left, but the whole thing had been bizarre. A man had never left her bed before, especially not to sleep on a couch. To be fair, the couch in her apartment couldn't fit a full-sized male, but something had been off. After her shower in the morning, Charlie had come right up to her and kissed her, but then been really distant the rest of the trip, even sneaking off to the couch again once she was asleep the next night.

The room seems fine to me, she'd thought. *Maybe he's uncomfortable with me menstruating? But he's a gynecologist. And he has four sisters. How can he be this weird about periods with four sisters?*

On the drive back from Montauk, Charlie had kept his window down the whole ride, only shutting it when it started to pour outside. The roar of the wind, later replaced by the drumming of the rain, kept them from talking most of the drive. They were less than an hour from her apartment when the rain let up, and he broke the ice.

"So I probably need to explain myself," said Charlie. The sky had been gray, and while the rain had stopped, the air inside the compartment was hot and sticky with humidity.

"I'd appreciate that," said Hunter.

"This is going to be uncomfortable," said Charlie. "Can I ask you what may seem like an uncomfortable question for a boyfriend to ask a girlfriend?" Air whooshed out of the car vents, blowing uncomfortably strong bursts of air.

"Yes," said Hunter softly, not knowing where this was going.

"Do you wash your genitals with regular soap?" The question hung in the air, and Hunter watched the leaf-laden trees twist in the wind.

"Of course I do. I'm a clean person," retorted Hunter. *Where is he going with this?* she thought. In truth, Hunter had only begun washing her genitals thoroughly a couple of weeks into her relationship with Charlie. She'd started washing because she was concerned her pussy would be below par for someone so well acquainted with the region. Before that, she'd figured her vulva cleaned itself. Originally, Hunter had used bar soap to wash her nether regions, then the week before the trip, she switched to using her new shampoo. The shampoo apparently contained silk, and though Hunter had no idea what silk smelled like, she thought it would make her scent luxurious.

"You're not supposed to wash your vulva or vagina with regular soap." Hunter squinted as Charlie continued, "Can I buy you some better soap? It's pH balanced."

Charlie stared straight at the road ahead, a steady three miles an hour over the speed limit. The lines were well demarcated, and Charlie stayed in the center of his lane as the road curved.

"I don't think I want that," said Hunter. "What's this about Charlie? Why did you sleep on the couch?" The wind picked up outside, and Hunter saw a tree double over with the gusts.

"To be honest, I couldn't sleep because of the smell," said Charlie.

"I thought that might be it," said Hunter with a small wave of relief hitting her. "Such a nice house, a shame if it smells bad. Not that it would bother me."

"No, Hunter, the smell is from your vagina. Like rotting fish. I was nauseous, and I didn't want to mention it while we were staying with my friends."

Rotting fish? thought Hunter. The relief turned to nausea. How could Charlie talk to her this way when he knew she was anosmic?

"Wow," had been all Hunter could say aloud.

"Oh Hunter, no, this isn't meant to be about you. This isn't your fault. You don't even have a sense of smell, but it is a problem."

Not about me? thought Hunter.

Charlie was still talking. "If women don't use the right pH balanced soap, then the bacteria colonies get out of balance and cause bad odor. The smell will typically increase around menstruation. The smell can get really bad, as in your case. I advise all my clients with smell issues to wash either with pH balanced soap or with no soap at all."

Now I'm a client with a smell issue? thought Hunter. She couldn't speak because her jaw was too clenched.

"I'll buy you the right soap, so you don't have to worry about it," said Charlie.

Hunter nodded in the car, but later, when he went to park outside her apartment, she'd asked to be dropped off. She wanted to be alone. Once she was inside her apartment, she texted Charlie, "Thanks for the weekend. I don't want the soap."

As Hunter lay in her bed, reflecting on their six-month relationship, her thoughts lingered on the Montauk trip and this exchange. Both had pretended the conversation hadn't happened on their next date.

Did he break up with me because I didn't want his vagina soap? She'd just been offended that he would say her vagina smelled like rotten fish and had refused the soap out of principle. *I don't want to think about vaginas anymore, and mine doesn't even work.*

That's when there was a noise from the intercom on the wall.

My pizza!

After buzzing the delivery driver in, Hunter grabbed some cash from the counter and her robe, which was lying on the ground, and threw it on. She then exited her apartment, standing on the small landing waiting for the driver to ascend the four flights of stairs to her apartment.

"Pizza for 5A?" he asked as he approached the landing. He was a thin, short man, made to look even smaller by the large pizza bag he carried.

"Yes, one large pineapple pizza." The two of them and the pizza barely both fit on the grimy landing.

"That's $23.10," he said. He bent over to unzip the pizza bag and sniffed the air noisily.

Hunter was counting the money when the delivery man began to cough.

"Are you okay?" she asked. He was still coughing. "Do you need some water?"

"No," he said between coughs. He was doubled over. The noise reverberated throughout the narrow stairwell. "Sorry," he managed to choke out. "This place. The smell. It's nasty," he continued between coughs.

Hunter trembled slightly as she attempted to hand the man $26. A nearby light fixture cast stark shadows on the scene.

"Thanks," the man said, clearing his throat as he handed her the pizza. "You should ask the building guy to check for a gas leak. They add stuff to the gas to make it smell like rotting eggs."

Holy shit, he's smelling my period.

Hunter said nothing as the man turned and hurried down the stairwell. His quick footsteps echoed anxiously.

Hunter went back into her apartment, holding the pizza box, and looked around her room. "This is a mess," she said out loud. Her appetite was gone. Putting the pizza box down carefully on one of the displaced couch cushions, Hunter went to the shower and rinsed off. She refused to use the silk shampoo and hadn't yet replaced it, so all she used was water. The inside of the shower curtain was covered in black furry patches.

Wow, Hunter, you need to get it together, or you'll always be alone on the holidays ordering shitty pizza.

Hunter got dressed and headed to Trader Joe's. It was only a few blocks away, and soon she had the requisite hand soap, dish soap, laundry soap, shampoo, body wash, conditioner, counter cleaner, and roll of paper towels. Next, she stopped at Bed Bath & Beyond, ostensibly to grab a new shower curtain.

After grabbing both a new shower curtain and a pack of shower curtain liners, Hunter continued to wander the store. That's when she found them: Summer's Eve and the Honey Pot vaginal wash. A month after the Montauk drive conversation, Hunter had gotten her period again and decided to google "vagina soap." The two brands had come up as options, but she'd quickly closed the browser thinking, *I am not the problem. His nose is the problem. I'm beautiful as I am.* But since then, her confidence had begun to crumble as the anger it was built on faded away. The pizza man was the final straw. This was now clearly her problem.

Hunter grabbed both bottles and put them in her cart before taking large strides to the checkout. As she walked out of the store and headed home, Hunter had one thought: *Maybe things didn't work out with Charlie, but never again is a man going to compare my genitals to any sort of rotting food item.*

Once home, Hunter began to clean. She took out the trash, put the sofa back together, washed the bowls in the sink, changed the shower curtain, washed the counter, emptied out her fridge and freezer of expired food, took out the garbage again, opened the window, and collected all her laundry off of the floor into a bag to bring to the laundromat, and even made her bed with the backup set of sheets.

This is the first time I've ever cleaned this place and no one's coming over. I guess this is for me. Wow.

The sheets on the bed were crisply folded, the couch looked inviting, and even the counters seemed to sparkle. A small wet patch remained on the carpet from where Hunter had attempted to get out the ice cream stain. Otherwise, everything was perfect. The apartment even felt bigger.

It was night now, and a smiling full moon peeked through her window and promised new beginnings. The passing lights of planes twinkled, and the breeze was gentle. After finally eating a room-temperature slice of pizza, Hunter went to shower again before bed. She read the instructions on her new shampoo, conditioner, body wash, and vaginal soap before using any of them.

Every speck of me is going to be clean. I guess what I'm thankful for this year is the opportunity to start fresh.

EPILOGUE

Throughout the book writing process, my editors have constantly assigned me checklists. Well-developed protagonist? Check! Appropriate tone for the story? Check! Now I'm at the epilogue, and shockingly there was no editor-assigned checklist. I found this unacceptably chaotic, so I made my own checklist below. I hope you don't mind me checking off a few more boxes before I let you go!

ONE: SUMMARIZE THE THEMES OF THE BOOK.

My dad always says (and don't sue him if this is plagiarized), "First you tell 'em what you're gonna tell 'em. Then you tell 'em. Then you tell 'em what you told 'em." This seems ridiculously repetitive but apparently necessary because you, the reader, may be daft. That's a joke. If you didn't get that was a joke, then maybe it wasn't a joke after all. Okay, now it's turned into a Schrodinger's cat of a joke, and I'm writing this at 1 a.m., and I think I'm hilarious.

Getting back to the point, the themes in this book centered around the diversity of circumstances and choices experienced by people who menstruate. These circumstances and choices can impact and be impacted by self-worth, family relationships, romantic relationships, friendships, values, physical health, mental health, the healthcare system, and more. I had a bucket full of potential themes, and rather than grabbing a handful, I grabbed the bucket and ran with it.

With so many themes, it is difficult to choose a single takeaway for this book. That's why I've charged myself with the difficult legwork of choosing a takeaway for you: "Love, Sleep, and Play." Wait, no, that's a Pampers ad campaign. Though, it's not the worst fit for this book. We should all start with "love" and treat our bodies right by getting enough "sleep." I could even turn "play" into a sex joke, but I probably shouldn't, given that the slogan started as a diapers ad, and I'm avoiding child pornography. Okay, where was I again? Ah yes, takeaways.

Lights… Drum roll… And now the takeaways I promised! If you take any lesson with you from this book, I hope it's how unique everyone's life experiences are. In this crazy world, the most you can do is support one another as best you can, accept that no one's perfect, and try to do your best. You are never stuck. You can always make different choices, except sometimes with health shit; that shit's terrifying! Everyone has their own challenges, and we usually don't know what others are going through (note the aforementioned terrifying health shit), so cut them some slack. Know that there are people in this world who are totally different than you, and that'ss okay. Choose to be someone you would love, and love yourself first. That's all you can do.

So yeah, instead of reading this book, you could have gotten all of these life lessons from reading cards at a Hallmark store. Sorry. Still, I'm glad you read my book, and I hope you are too! It's always good to flex the empathy muscle. Also, let's be honest, it's been fun! A lot more fun than reading greeting cards would have been. And now you can brag to your friends about reading an artsy book about menstruation. That's pretty fit.

☑ Check!

TWO: ACKNOWLEDGE THE LIMITATIONS OF THE BOOK.
It's important to acknowledge what this book could and could not accomplish. Writing this book, I attempted to build a collage reflecting the diversity of experiences people have around menstruation.

While I was able to cover many stories, weaving fact and fiction into a form of story-truth, I was unable to use everything shared with me in the interviews I completed as research for this book. This is always true for authors, but for me, there was an added factor. Many of the stories I chose not to include in the final book were those I didn't want to risk representing inaccurately. For those who spoke to me about serious medical conditions and wrought relationships (often involving family), your stories were heard and valued. I hope someday everyone can hear these stories told with the deference they deserve.

A book will never replace listening to the stories of the people in your own life. Obviously, don't interrogate strangers on a train about their first time menstruating (unless you're in some weird Indie rom-com movie moment), but chatting with close friends should always be okay. If you want, you can even use this book as an ice breaker! Not a literal ice breaker (while mentally sharp, this book is physically quite dull and would not easily break the ice), instead more of a, "Hey friendo, I read this truly incredible and monumentally inspiring book called *Period? Life with Menstruation*. *I don't want to put you on the spot, but if you ever have any period stories you want to share or if you want to vent about how tampons are taxed in the US, then I'm totally here to listen!"* Give that a go, or maybe something similar, and you could learn something incredible.

P.S. I also have an entire list of scenarios that didn't make this book. If you want to ghostwrite the sequel for me, the list is ready to go! A couple of fun list items included menstrual cups pulling out IUDs (always break the menstrual cup seal before pulling it out), and going through the technological advancements in pads over time (they used to have belts)!

☑ Check!

THREE: THANK THE READER.

Thank you, dear reader, for taking your time and your mental bandwidth to read this book all the way through to the epilogue. Thank you from the depths of my soul for powering through over 50,000 words about vaginas, women, and the human experience. As a squeamish human myself, I know how difficult it can be to work through the topics we covered in this book. You could have waited for the audiobook version to come out (hopefully, Emma Watson will narrate, but Emma Stone or David Tennant would be equally fabulous). But you didn't. You read this paperback (or eBook) cover to cover, one word at a time. What I'm trying to say is, thank you for supporting my effort to break down the taboos around menstruation using humor and humility. Coming on this journey with me required commitment and demonstrated good values (since we both know you didn't read this book for the limited laughs). Know that I strive to be more like you.

☑ Check!

FOUR: THANK THE AMAZING PEOPLE WHO SUPPORTED THIS BOOK.

Normally this section would be a separate chapter called "acknowledgments," but I'm not going to do that. Given how integral the people who supported this book were to its publication, it's important to me to incorporate them into the substance of the book here in the epilogue. They did a lot of heavy emotional and financial lifting, and they deserve a solid shout-out.

So many marvelous folks let me interview them or contributed to this book in other ways, and I wouldn't be done without thanking some directly. Some preferred to remain anonymous, which I totally respect. For those who didn't mind me shouting their names from the rooftops, I'd like to thank as many as I can. Get ready for a lot of thank yous to some of the best people on the planet. (Note that you, reader, are likely also one of the best people on this planet, but I've already thanked you in the previous item.)

Thank you to my inspiring interviewees: Adam Raphael, Anne Lazenby, Arianna Mathioudakis, Ashwini Arvind, Charlotte Weiss, Claire Sinai, Currin Hall, Katherine Evans, Kezi Cheng, Michelle Chao, Rachel Neubert, Rozz Mandel, Sarah Beller, and many more who preferred to remain anonymous! I could not have written this book without you all! As a reminder to readers, all of the stories in the book are fiction, but they were directly inspired by the experiences of these and many other real women (and nonwomen).

Thank you, Margaret Danko, my Developmental Editor, for steering me clear of accidental child pornography, general pornography, racism, sexism, and general bad stuff I would not want in my book. Also, thank you for spinning my wacky stories about exploding menstrual cups into tales of the human condition. You went totally beyond what I ever could have hoped for in a Developmental Editor, as I knew you would be from the moment you started talking about vagina-scented candles.

Thank you, Carol McKibben, my Marketing and Revisions Editor, for your positivity and help finding direction in some of the lost sections. You helped me find my way.

Thank you, Eric Koester, for having the best book writing class I could have ever stumbled into and for not even flinching as I gave you my book proposal all about vaginas and blood. Your class was excellent, and I truly admire your spoken words per minute.

Thank you, Haley Newlin, for being an excellent teacher and enthusiast. Every horror-based example you gave was a delight.

Thank you, Golara Haghtalab, for being my accountability buddy. You are an incredible cheerleader, and even if I hadn't been fortunate enough to get this book published, your friendship would have been enough of a reward (almost). Shout out for your upcoming book! It's going to be incredible!

Thank you, Harrison Weisberg, for being my favorite butt face in the entire world. Oh, and also for feeding me when I was cranky while writing this book. You're an excellent cook and an excellent boyfriend. Also, as of recently, an excellent fiancé. It's been a wild ride over the last six years, and

I wouldn't change a thing. Okay, maybe since I was in the middle of writing this book, I would have paid for a moving company to relocate us halfway across the country, but I definitely wouldn't change you. I love you, and I love us.

Thank you, Lori Prosnitz, my mom and my editor since I began writing, for taking the time to go through my entire book with me. Your endless support has meant the world to me. You make me a better writer and a better person.

Thank you, David Prosnitz, my dad, for genuinely trying to talk about the spirituality of menstrual blood after I told you I was writing this book. It's incredible how much you care. You inspire me to work hard and build from the ground up.

Thank you, Joseph Prosnitz, my brother, for spreading my period message around the globe. I appreciate how you try and support me in every way you know how.

Thank you, Hannah Eckstein, my sister, for teaching me so many things in life, from mascara to shaving. When I asked you about referencing you in the introduction, you told me that it was my book and you'd support me in my creativity. You've always had my back like that.

Did you participate in the presale? I haven't forgotten about you! Without your financial support, this book would never have been published. You covered the cost of an incredible team of editors and designers who made this book shine! *Thank you!* You've come from all corners of my life: childhood, college, adult life, and more. Some of you are literal strangers from the internet (shoutout to Imgur!). Yet you all came together to support me and to support breaking down the taboos around menstruation. That's truly incredible.

Presale contributors:

- Adam Raphael and Currin Hall

- Aditya Mahajan
- Albin Anthony
- Alex Mark
- Alexandria Byer
- Alice Abousleiman
- Allison Newell
- Amanda Cohen
- Anika Huhn
- Anissa Wong and Kelsey Robinson
- Anna Calamaro
- Anne Hillebrand
- Anne Lazenby
- Annie and Adam
- Annie LaBine
- Annie Perrotti
- Annie Whalen
- Arianna Mathioudakis
- Arielle Friedler
- Arvind Gautam
- Ashley Mauler
- Ashley Perry
- Ashley Sorensen
- Ashwini Arvind
- Austin and Alice Zielman
- Bailey Eckersley
- Barbara Schloss
- Benjamin Jacobson
- Breanna Bartlett
- Brendan Cottam
- Briana Morey
- Bruno Faviero
- Bryan Woodruff

- Carmelle Benishay
- Carol Dyson
- Carolyn Sinai
- Cary DeMello
- Cathy Levin
- Cera Xenapus Leavis
- Charlotte Weiss
- Claire Sinai
- Cori Drysdale
- Corianne Randstrom
- Dalton Ryan
- Dana Kobylenski
- Danielle Cloutier
- David Bezalel Flamholz
- Dayton Faraco
- Elana Ben-Akiva
- Elisabeth Rosen
- Elise Kuo
- Elizabeth West
- Emily Valdez
- Emma Lichtenstein
- Eric Jaffe
- Eric Koester
- Erin Bishop
- Erin Staples
- Evan Goldstein
- Ewan and Chloe Riley
- Gabriella Meltzer
- Golara Haghtalab
- Gregory Burlingame
- Gurmeet Kaur
- Halliki Voolma

- Hannah Eckstein
- Harrison Erik Weisberg
- Ian Gaft-Azcue
- Inbar and Max Plaut
- Jacqueline Urick
- James Baker
- James Eckersley
- James Larson
- Janelle Mansfield
- Jelena Cvitanovic
- Jenn Tilton
- Jennifer D Weisberg
- Jennifer Tang
- Jodi Pavia
- Jon Reilly
- Jonathan Go
- Joseph Prosnitz
- Joseph Roy-Mayhew
- Josh Lipschultz
- Julia
- Juliana Abramovich
- Julie Finkelstein
- Kaitlyn Cruz
- Karen Lobl Eisenberg
- Kat and Alex
- Katherine Evans
- Katherine Payette
- Katherine Scarpellini
- Kathryn Schumacher
- Keren Schmahmann
- Kezi Cheng
- Kirrah Jones

- Lee Gross
- Lee Nissim
- Lori Prosnitz
- Louisa Antonelli
- Luis F Voloch
- Madeleine Bairey
- Maggie Su
- Manuela Zoninsein
- Margaret Hillyard-Lazenby
- Mason Cooper
- Matthew Susskind
- Max Weisberg
- Maya S Patel
- Melissa Goldberg
- Michelle Chao
- Michelle Dutt
- Milana Bochkur Dratver
- Nam Le
- Nancy Lu
- Naomi Stark
- Nathan Eamon Colgan
- Nicholas Germinario
- Nicholas Sondej
- Nizar Dahbar
- Noa Ghersin
- Omar Trujillo
- Ori Weisberg
- Parikshit Dey
- Paul Larochelle
- Pete Falcone
- Priya and Dip
- Rachel Neubert

- Rebecca Dall'Orso
- Rebecca Joey Schwab
- Rebecca Levin
- Richard Savoia
- Robert Hollister
- Robin Goettel
- Rosalyn C. Mandel
- Ryan Fantus
- Sam O'Connor
- Sana Chintamen
- Sarah Beller
- Sarah Horton
- Sarah Toledano
- Sarah Wilson
- Sean Michael Cumming
- Shreeja Basak
- Sofiya Teplitskaya
- Stephanie Williams
- Tally Portnoi
- Tara Hicks
- Taylor Pearl
- Tessa Green
- Tiffany Wong
- Timothy Mansfield
- Tobi Rudoltz
- Veronica Puistonen

And for my penultimate thank you, I want to thank myself.

Miriam, you're marvelous. Writing this book has been the biggest thing you've probably ever done. Take a moment to celebrate that. Sometimes it's so easy to skip over the self-love (surprisingly not a double entendre) and self-compassion. Don't do that. While writing this book, you worked through a global pandemic, a day job, medical issues, planning a move, actually moving cross-country, loss, starting graduate school, and a lot more. Don't forget that. Love and appreciate yourself. You deserve it.

While that's only the surface of people I want to and should thank, I'm running out of words. To everyone in my life not named directly above, you've still contributed tremendously to this book. Every offhand conversation and little idea nugget came from the experiences of real people who were kind enough to share them with me. Thank you for existing and being a part of my life.

☑ Check!

FIVE: PUT A BOW ON IT AND CALL IT A NIGHT.

Wow, I can't believe this is it. I'm having a hard time letting go, but I think it's important to let things end and appreciate them for what they've given us.

After reading this book, I hope the next time you meet someone that you take the time to ask for their stories. Maybe don't ask everyone (maybe skip asking your work colleagues about vaginas, so you don't end up in an HR report), but be curious and be open to the world. Everyone has experiences, and we're all unique. Tell your story! Listen to others share theirs. Build community together. Make this world shine like a beautiful mosaic.

☑ Check!

THE END.

APPENDIX

———

AUTHOR'S NOTE

Samaritans USA. "History of Samaritans." 2010. http://www.samaritansusa.org/history.php.